Best wishes always to ~~them~~ A~~ll~~
with love from all of us,
to you and all your loved ones,
Enjoy my second book in
good Health and Happiness,
Love always
Dad

IN SEARCH
OF SELF,
IN THE
SERVICE
OF OTHERS

IN SEARCH
OF SELF,
IN THE
SERVICE
OF OTHERS

Reflections of a
Retired Physician
on Medicine, the
Bible, & the Jews

HEINZ
HARTMANN, M.D.

 Prometheus Books

59 John Glenn Drive
Amherst, New York 14228-2197

Published 1998 by Prometheus Books

02 01 00 99 98   5 4 3 2 1

Library of Congress Cataloging-in-Publication Data

Hartmann, Heinz, 1913–
    In search of self, in the service of others : reflections of a retired physician
on medicine, the Bible & the Jews / by Heinz Hartmann.
        p.   cm.
    Includes bibliographical references.
    ISBN 1–57392–230–7 (cloth : alk. paper)
    1. Hartmann, Heinz, 1913–   . 2. Jews, German—New York
(State)—Syracuse—Biography. 3. Physicians—New York (State)—
Syracuse—Biography. 4. Jews—Germany—Biography. 5. Jews—
Germany—History—1933–1945. 6. Syracuse (N.Y.)—Biography. I. Title.
F129.S8H24   1998
974.7′66004924′0092—dc21
        [B]   98–29224
                                                                              CIP

Printed in the United States of America on acid-free paper

To Herta

1912 to 1988

Everyone who knew her, loved her.

Contents

Introduction

After the publication of my autobiographical volume, *Once a Doctor, Always a Doctor: The Memoirs of a German-Jewish Immigrant Physician,* in 1986-87, I was sure that I had expressed my most important thoughts on my life, my work, my family, and my friends. I hadn't the faintest desire to write a subsequent volume. As I told one reviewer, "What can be a sequel to one's own life?"

But in the decade or more that has passed since I penned those thoughts, my world has changed dramatically. Most particularly, I lost my dear wife, Herta, to the ravages of cancer in 1988. Not only did she demonstrate the stamina and courage that saw her through so many struggles during our life together, but in her waning days and weeks she showed all of us how to hold on to life and how extraordinarily graceful and dignified one's departing can be.

In *Once a Doctor* I introduced readers to our physically disabled and mentally retarded son, Michael. Since the earliest months of his existence, Michael's life has been a series of obstacles—more than most people could bear—yet he manages to make the most of each day. But as you will see, both

9

Michael and I would face even bigger challenges in the years ahead. I would be forced to make one of the most difficult decisions of my life.

Now that I am well into my eighties, I have become far more reflective—more introspective—and desirous of understanding my place in the world. This has prompted me to ponder my role as husband, father, and grandfather within my family and to explore the deeper meaning of my life as a friend, community member, doctor, Holocaust survivor, and, most fundamentally, as a Jew. But if I have learned nothing else in my life during these decades of reading, reflecting, and searching for the self that is me, I firmly believe that these aspects of who and what I am cannot be explored separately. They must be viewed at one and the same time as individual threads which the direction and focus of my life have woven into a rich tapestry, each fiber of which would not be what it is or where it is if viewed in isolation from all the others.

When pondering my experiences and those of other Jews in Nazi Germany, and the Jewish mandate to heal the world in the hope of a better future for all, I am reminded of the words of the old Negro spiritual, "We Shall Overcome." I will have occasion to return to similar thoughts, especially when discussing the relationship of Judaism to other religious and non-religious beliefs.

And in exploring what makes me who I am I find that my search for self begins and ends in service to others. . . .

1

Moving On

It was in the early part of 1981 that Herta felt a tiny lump in her breast. When the biopsy came back positive for the presence of cancer, she underwent a modified radical mastectomy, performed by Dr. Daniel Burdick. There were no malignant lymphnodes found and the tumor had apparently not spread. While this was very good news, indeed, Herta still had to undergo a number of radiation treatments. Three years after the mastectomy, she felt another lump on the chestwall of her right breast. Dr. Burdick prescribed Tamoxifen, an anti-estrogen drug in the hope of reducing the lump by limiting the hormone estrogen that was stimulating it. In October 1987, due to a sudden bout of severe anemia, a bone marrow biopsy was performed by her oncologist, Dr. Robert Smith. The biopsy showed the infiltration of breast cancer cells into the bone marrow.

In addition to her cancer, Herta had to be treated for her diabetic condition. Under the guidance of Dr. Philip Speller, an endocrinologist, I checked my wife's bloodsugar daily and gave her the required insulin injection. Even with her various treatments, Herta grew steadily weaker, and it became harder for her to move around without help. But through it all, she

11

always new that we loved her and that we were there for her. One day she was watching a soap opera at the kitchen table and she seemed to be holding her head up with her hands. Our grandson, Maurice, entered the room and asked, "Grandma, why do you have to hold your head with your hands?" She simply replied, "I am just tired."

Stomach and intestinal symptoms soon occurred, in part due to the various medications Herta was taking. One day, when Dr. Burdick made one of his home visits to see her (What a rare doctor he was!), she blurted out: "Sometimes, with all this trouble I have, I think I must have AIDS." Dr. Burdick chuckled and replied, "Herta, AIDS is one thing I can assure you that you haven't got."

In spite of the seriousness of Herta's illness we were not dismayed. We always had a positive attitude thanks to two of Dr. Bernie Siegel's books: *Love, Medicine and Miracles* and *Peace, Love, and Healing.* Although Herta, unfortunately, was already in the final stages of her illness, I have always kept in mind what Dr. Siegel expressed so well in his writings: that the mental and spiritual attitude of the patient will promote healing even in the most obstinate cases in which the patient is told by the doctor that he or she has only a few months to live. In numerous instances, according to Dr. Siegel, these patients were still living years later, thus showing the physicians just how wrong they had been with their pessimistic prognoses. I was delightfully surprised to receive two personal notes from Dr. Siegel, mailed from his Connecticut office, advising me that he had received a copy of my book *Once a Doctor,* with the possibility that he might review it if time permitted. Unfortunately, that review never occurred.

In September of 1987, Herta participated in the bar mitzvah celebration of our grandson, Maurice Raichelson, at the Reformed Temple Society of Concord, Syracuse, New York. Later on, family, friends, and many of our relatives were there, including Herta's sister Lucy, who would be celebrating her ninetieth birthday the same month. All of the out-of-town relatives were either from California (those from Herta's side) or from Canada (my side of the family). It was remarkable how on these rare occasions when the whole family attempts to be together, both my family and Herta's interact as if they had known each other all their lives. It was not easy for Herta to attend such family gatherings, however festive they might be, but she looked forward so much to each event and was happy not to have missed Maurice's big day.

In the following weeks my dear wife grew still weaker. Eventually, she was unable to manipulate the electric controls for her reclining chair. As a matter of fact, two of us had to lift her and walk with her whenever she had to take a few steps. To make matters worse, Herta developed increased jaundice with all of its side effects of itching, nausea, and general malaise. Dr. Burdick came to the house again, this time to convince Herta that she should be hospitalized. But she didn't want to leave the home she loved. Finally, on December 7, 1987, she was admitted to Crouse Irving Memorial Hospital.

At the hospital Herta was surgically supervised by Dr. Herbert Mendel. He told us from the start that she had about five or six weeks to live and that the hospital would take care of all her needs. It was quite a shock. Needless to say, we didn't believe the doctor at first. We were sure that a miracle would happen and she would be fine.

Herta's most pressing problem upon admission was the obstructive jaundice. Dr. Ajoy Roy, one of the consultants, did an endoscopic examination of the gallbladder ducts, which showed a common bile duct obstruction due to the pressure of a pancreatic cancer. Following this more exact diagnosis, percutaneous drainage with a transhepatic catheter was undertaken by Dr. Gerald Black, a specialist in advanced medical imaging. It allowed the bile to drain into an outside vessel, instead of continuing to seep into her bloodstream causing the toxic juandiced condition. "It is like a miracle," Herta told me when her yellow face started to clear up and many other symptoms subsided. I was surprised and grateful at how Dr. Black always took the time to explain each medical procedure and what it would do to improve the quality of Herta's remaining days and weeks. It was encouraging to have a consultant in the field of radiology who gave so much of his time to communicate with each patient's family. In this day and age of fast-paced medical advances and concern over the cost of care, it's encouraging to know that a few caring physicians exist.

Herta's troubles were not over. She developed an accumulation of fluid on her lungs, due to the spread of cancer cells. The fluid caused some shortness of breath. Eventually, she developed congestive heart failure, but she was always given the proper medication when the discomfort reached beyond her level of tolerance. I only heard her complain once, when she remarked: "I never knew how much one has to suffer before one goes." Our daughter, Joan Raichelson, asked Dr. J. R. Smith, the oncologist, in the final days of Herta's illness: "Does she know she is going to die?"

"Of course she does," he replied. "She grows weaker every day. She has always been a nurse . . . she knows."

Herta knew.

All of us—Joan; her husband, Mel; myself; and the grandchildren, Sarah and Maurice, were with Herta during her hospital stay—whenever it was humanly possible. Once, when Eleene Seeber, a dear friend of the family for over thirty years, came to pay Herta a visit, my wife asked Eleene right away, "Who takes care of Michael?" There was always a home aide at the house with our disabled son.

Rabbi Theodore Levy, now rabbi emeritus of Temple Society of Concord, visited and talked with Herta frequently, and from time to time some of our many friends stayed with her over night. Among these kind and generous people were: Barbara Lillis; Esther Porter, daughter of our long-time friend, Rita Seligman; and Esther's son, Kenny. During the last stage of Herta's terminal illness, it was decided that Joan and I would alternate spending the night with her. One of us would rest on a cot while every hour on the hour those especially wonderful nurses would enter the room to check Herta's pulse, blood pressure and respiration, and administer medication when indicated. One morning, when Dr. Burdick paid Herta a hospital visit, after I had spent the night at her side, she asked, "Don't I have a nice husband?"

"You sure have," he replied.

When my spirits get low at times, I only have to think of that short conversation and I feel uplifted.

During Herta's last night, after she had received her prescribed sedation, Joan stayed with her. Herta died in the early morning hours of January 10, 1988. It was Joan's birthday. Both Joan and I felt that Herta wanted to cling to life just until the official start of her only daughter's birthday. That same day, in Herta's room, when we were saying our last goodbyes, the nurses and aides would come over to us, some with tears in their eyes, and hug us. Apparently, they had never seen a terminal patient who was visited and cared for by loved ones as much as Herta was. All too often a certain point is reached in an illness and the relatives don't seem to know how to communicate anymore. At this point families and friends often distance themselves from their loved one—just when the patient needs them the most.

An interdenominational service for our Herta was arranged by Crouse Irving Hospital. It was a great help to all of us.

There were many people from all walks of life at Herta's funeral: friends from India, China, Italy, and Germany attended, as well as our relatives from Canada—represented by our cousin Inge Spitz of Toronto—while Mary Ann from Sunnyvale, California, brought along a wonderful and loving prayer which was read from the pulpit by Rabbi Levy. It was written by Herta's older sister, Lucy van der Linde, who used to visit or travel with us every year for decades. My friend Ken Walton, who attended school with me in Germany over seventy years ago, came from Rochester, New York, with his wife, Paula. Ken assured us that he had never heard such an eloquent eulogy as the one given for Herta by Rabbi Levy. At our request, Rabbi Levy sent us a copy of that eulogy, and we reread it from time to time on special occasions. As Rabbi Sheldon Ezring, the present rabbi of the Temple Society of Concord, once told his congregation, "As long as we remember our departed loved ones, that is the surest way to know that they have an afterlife."

Did we do everything that is right for Herta? Did we show her how much we loved her? I was completely reassured when I listened on one of the following Sundays to Reverend Robert Schuller's message from his Crystal Cathedral in Garden Grove, California. In contrast to most of the fundamentalist preachers, he had on his program Jewish Holocaust survivors and famous Jewish personalities such as the Vienna-born psychiatrist Victor Frankl, a person Dr. Schuller considered one of his heroes. That particular Sunday his guest was Dr. Bernie Siegel, who told the congregation that in the terminal stage of an illness, when you show love to your family member, that is something very special, a unique bonding between you and the patient that no one can take away from you. It made me feel good to hear this from an expert.

         &   &   &

Herta was there for me when I wrote the manuscript for my autobiographical volume. She helped me to remember and at times to correct many recollections. I only sent the project to a few publishers. Before starting *Once a Doctor,* I had written reviews for the *Syracuse Jewish Observer.* I started to write for the *Observer* in the early 1980s under its editor, Sherry Chayat, who is now writing about art in *Stars* magazine. I continue to write reviews for the *Observer* under its present editor, Mollie Leitzes Collins.

I remember vividly the first book I ever reviewed for the *Syracuse Jewish Observer.* It was a three-volume biography titled *Martin Buber's Life and Work* by the philosopher Maurice Friedman. It made me feel good to see how many people benefited from this and other reviews of mine. It gave me the courage to begin work on my own story. I recall, that soon after my report on the Buber biography I was contacted by Dr. Samuel Mallov, a professor of pharmacology, who intended to purchase the Buber work for his son, an internist in Indianapolis. I continued to communicate with the professor, seeing him at meetings and corresponding with him until his death about four years ago.

So, after writing my autobiography, I sent the manuscript to several publishers, but each one felt that my work did not fit their present publishing program. The plight of first authors is a frustrating one: no publisher likes to take the risk of accepting the work of someone new and unknown. Then I remembered Dr. Paul Kurtz, with whom I had corresponded once in the late seventies. Kurtz, then a professor of philosophy at the State University of New York at Buffalo, had just left the well-established intellectual magazine *The Humanist* to start a new secular humanist publication which he named *Free Inquiry.* Kurtz was also editor of Prometheus Books, then in its fifteenth year. When I sent him the manuscript of "Once a Doctor," he agreed to publish my little volume, calling it a "fine book."

Prometheus Books published *Once a Doctor, Always a Doctor* in the latter part of 1986. Gradually, fine reviews started to pour in: the *Journal of the History of Medicine,* the *Midwest Book Review, Aufbau* in New York, *The Jerusalem Post* (Syracuse), the *Star's* Sunday magazine, and the *Syracuse Jewish Observer,* among others. Since I practiced for about four years in Tully, New York, and was known to that community, Walter Grunfeld, editor of the *Independent Villager,* came to my house for a long interview and wrote a very detailed and interesting story about me. He had even taken a picture of me and my granddaughter, Sarah, while he was with us. Mr. Grunfeld, by the way, is also a German-Jewish immigrant, but he left Nazi Germany as a boy and came to the United States after attending school in England.

Before Mr. Grunfeld left, I showed him a report that my twelve-year-old grandson, Maurice, had written on my book.* A short time later, Mr. Grunfeld returned to take a picture of my grandson together with his mother (my daughter) Joan. He

---

*Later Maurice was enrolled as a student at Cortland College, Cortland, New York, and then graduated from Syracuse University.

also reprinted Maurice's review in the *Independent Villager* under the title "A Grandson Comments on His Grandfather's Book." I would feel remiss if I didn't share with you Maurice's review:

Once a Doctor, Always a Doctor:
The Memoirs of a German Jewish Immigrant Physician

by Heinz Hartmann, M.D.
(my grandfather)

My report is about a courageous man named Heinz Hartmann, M.D. Born in Ostrow, Prussia, in 1913, he is still much alive today. My story begins with a young medical student of non-Aryan descent who hardly escaped Nazi Germany with his life.

As a student my grandfather was surrounded with the terror of watching all his loved ones being shipped off to concentration camps. His hometown also was in the middle of vandalizing Jewish stores and looting of homes. His favorite musicians couldn't play his favorite songs because of Jewish discrimination. My grandfather had no choice but to go to Berne, Switzerland, if he intended to become a doctor. Later he returned with his medical degree to work and to practice at a local hospital, where he met Herta (my grandmother), a young nurse who was scared to give shots (that's how they met). Latter they got married and planned on going to the Land of Promise where freedom was guaranteed, the US of A.

Unfortunately, before they could complete their plan, Dr. Hartmann was shipped off to Buchenwald. His newlywed wife (two weeks after their marriage) progressed in her nursing work, thinking her husband was dead. She would often lie to others saying patients were very sick, dying, or diseased so they, too, would not have to go to a concentration camp. Luckily my grandfather made it out of that prison in 1938 but also luckily he was only six to seven weeks imprisoned in Buchenwald. He soon found his wife and after very complicated, dangerous, and expensive planning they escaped from Europe to come to America.

There are many more interesting stories and funny poems and events in this book. It is a very good book (because I am in it) and I'll read it again any time. All in all, *Once a Doctor, Always a Doctor* is a book about adventure in Nazi Germany and other trials in America including his handicapped son, Michael.

I hope you read a copy soon!

Maurice Raichelson

I was very much impressed with some of the other book reviews I received. I had sent a copy of my book to Rabbi Dr. Albert Friedlander in London, England, who is now editor of *European Judaism.* He is also the author of *Out of the Whirlwind: A Reader of Holocaust Literature, Leo Baeck of Theresienstadt,* and, among others, *A Thread of Gold: Journeys towards Reconciliation.* He sent me a heartwarming note of recommendation for my book, which he allowed me to use freely.

Knowing that my autobiography was to be, to the best of my knowledge, the only one written by a Jewish refugee physician, I quite naturally thought very highly of my work. Each week for several weeks I would check the book review section of the *New York Times,* but no review of my book ever appeared. Finally, I contacted Ann Roiphe, the well-known novelist who, a few years earlier, had written her *Generation without Memory,* describing her interest in and return to Judaism. Many times I had seen her reviews about similar topics, so I asked her to consider writing something about my autobiography. *The New York Times* was nice enough to forward my request to her. She indicated in her beautiful reply that she was not able to send in a review unless requested to do so by the editors of the paper. She wished me all the best.

There was yet another time when the *New York Times* helped me. On April 12, 1987, there appeared an article in the *New York Times* magazine by Suzanne M. Batzdorff titled "A Martyr of Auschwitz," telling about her Aunt Edith Stein, originally from Breslau, who later converted to Catholicism and became a nun. She used the name Sister Teresa-Benedicta. She died, unfortunately, under the Nazis at Auschwitz. Mrs. Batzdorff, her husband, and about twenty other relatives had been invited to Cologne to attend her Aunt Edith's beatification ceremony. I remembered right away that, during my days in Breslau, I knew Mrs. Batzdorff's father, Dr. Biberstein, a dermatologist, as well as her father-in-law, Dr. Batzdorff, a surgeon. I wrote a letter to the editor of the *New York Times* magazine making some remark with regard to her article and mentioning the fact that I remembered her above-mentioned relations in Breslau. My letter was not printed, though it was forwarded to Mrs. Batzdorff in Santa Rosa, California. We have exchanged books and have been in contact ever since.

Suzanne Batzdorff wrote similar articles about her Aunt Edith in several other magazines: *Moment, Aufbau,* and the *Jewish Spectator.* I sent a letter of response to these periodicals and was published, sometimes in shortened form. Mrs. Batzdorff went with her husband, Alfred, to Cologne with mixed feelings. She and all of her other relatives are sure that Sister Teresa died in Auschwitz as a Jewess, regardless of her conversion, while the Catholic Church maintains that the motive of the Nazi action was "hatred against the church." Still, in spite of her misgivings she collaborates in her research on her Aunt Edith with nuns and other Catholic personalities, here and abroad. I was very much impressed with her work titled *Edith Stein: Selected Writings,* published in 1990 by Templegate. The last chapter of these writings bears the title "Catholics and Jews: Can We Bridge the Abyss?" It offers so many common sense ideas that a few passages are worthy of being quoted:

> The job of achieving understanding between Christians and Jews must be ongoing. . . . It will not help to declare that differences between the faiths are unimportant, that there is really only one "Judeo-Christian ideology." Edith's choice to become a Catholic was a blow because of what Chris-

tianity had done to the Jews in the past. Her entry into Carmel came at a moment when the Jews were threatened by Christians as never before. . . . The irony and tragedy of Edith Stein's life was that in following her conscience on the road to Christianity she felt that she was pursuing her Jewish past to its ultimate goal. But it is impossible, from the Jewish perspective, to see it that way. For Jews, the Christian faith is not the natural culmination of Judaism, but another path, another truth. We cannot accept the thesis that "the Old Covenant is fulfilled in the New." . . . Judaism is a religious entity, a system of beliefs and teachings that carries its own fulfillment, its own messianic goals and hopes. And thus a Jew who turns to Catholicism, in my view, is no longer a Jew. . . . Edith Stein tells us that by becoming a Catholic she felt truly Jewish for the first time in her life, but to her Jewish family it appeared that she had left the fold. . . .

I have had occasion to quote from Mrs. Batzdorff's book many times; her sentiments are so much in agreement with my own. She gave me permission to do so several years ago, after her selected writings were published.

At this point I would like to repeat a story I originally reported in *Once a Doctor, Always a Doctor*: On one of Phil Donahue's talk show episodes featuring politics and religion, Phil asked a young fundamentalist Christian girl whether she thought that a Jew who led an exemplary life could expect to get to heaven. The girl, visibly embarrassed, hemmed and hawed but finally blurted out that the Jew would have to go to hell. The Bible told her so. She saw no discrepancy between a loving religion and such a harsh God.

Those of you who read my earlier book may also remember my neighbor Louis De Stefano. Quite a few years ago his saintly wife, Jenny, now deceased, explained to me that she came from a large family of thirteen. "Did Louis also come from such a large family?" I asked. "Oh, no!" she exclaimed. "Only nine."

Louis told me sometime later that as a young boy in

Catholic Sunday school he was told by a priest that only Catholics go to heaven. He was afraid to speak up, but he always wondered how this could be. How could a merciful God allow a decent person to burn in hell just because that person is of a different faith?

It must be said, though, that since the pontificate of Pope John XXIII and under the present Pope John Paul II, things have changed. The Catholic Church no longer blames the Jews of today for the death of Jesus, and it declares that a Jew, or anyone who has not converted to Christianity, can find salvation in his Judaism. The same good will is shown to the Jewish people by many conservative though nonfundamentalist Protestant churches. If only this attitude would have been shown by the religious authorities centuries earlier, much unnecessary bloodshed and persecution could have been avoided. As we have been told since childhood by our Jewish writings, "The righteous of all nations have a share in the world to come!"

I was still in medical practice when *Once a Doctor, Always a Doctor* appeared in print. Medicaid patients would purchase it and bring their copies to their scheduled appointments so I could inscribe them. Those poor people didn't mind at all paying for a hardcover volume. I was not so lucky with my private patients. "I'll wait until it comes out in paperback or to the libraries," many said. Though it has not come out in paperback, most of the libraries in my area carry it and have invited me to read from it occasionally. As a matter of fact, my book is now available all over the country as well from libraries overseas, due to the fact that the Association of Jewish Libraries, with branches and members all over the world, through its vice president for publications, saw to it that most of the libraries received a copy. They recommend my memoirs as Holocaust reading for adolescents and adults. Mrs. Helen Guttenplan, our Temple Society of Concord librarian, notified me of this great honor. She always keeps two copies of my book in her library, one of the biggest Jewish libraries in Syracuse and central New York.

At the conservative synagogue Temple Adath Yeshurun,

Rabbi Charles Sherman gave my book a very warm review in July of 1987 during his Friday night service, which he dubbs "Services Under the Stars." I sent him my autobiography after hearing him talk about his disabled son, Eyal, a quadriplegic whose existence is maintained by a respirator and feeding tubes. He needs round-the-clock nursing. The boy was diagnosed with a brain tumor at a local hospital in March of 1986. He was just five and a half years old at the time, and Rabbi Sherman and his wife, Leah, were told by the doctors that their son had only a few weeks to live. They just could not bring themselves to accept that verdict, so they took Eyal to New York University Hospital with the help of a large Christian organization. Their son was operated on by Dr. Fred Epstein, the head of New York University's Division of Pediatric Neurosurgery. The title of Rabbi Sherman's book is *There Are No Atheists in the Intensive Care Unit.*

Dr. Epstein still checks on Eyal from time to time in Syracuse. Eyal is not able to speak, but with lip reading and the help of a computer he is able to express himself and to do his school work. On June 11, 1996, he celebrated his bar mitzvah.

🐿   🐿   🐿

When my friend Fred S. Preuss (from my high school days in Breslau, Germany) and his wife, Sonia, invited me to San Antonio in 1988, he had made arrangements for me to speak about my book before the local B'nai Brith organization. During my visit, Fred and Sonia took me to the libraries, museums, and exhibitions and showed me again the historical sites of San Antonio. But what I remember most is a conversation we had in the car.

"How many copies of your book have you sold so far?" Fred asked me.

"Several hundred copies," I estimated.

"That's pretty good," he replied.

"Pretty good? Some authors sell a million copies right away," I pointed out.

"But these books will be forgotten, when yours will still be available," he said.

I have no idea if Fred remembers this conversation, but I do.

♣   ♣   ♣

A little while later, by arrangement with my literary agent, Trudy Garfunkel of Kew Gardens, New York, I was invited to read from my memoir at the large Jewish Community Center in Rochester, New York. While in Rochester, I spent several days at the home of Ken and Paula Walton as their guest. Ken had been an elementary schoolmate of mine in Breslau. My book pictured them attending my seventieth birthday party. In the same picture is another school friend from those days so long ago, Erwin Zadik and his wife, Ursula, both of the Bronx. I correspond with them on a regular basis.

During the days I stayed at Ken and Paula Walton's home, I told them a story about Milton Kamen, a frequent guest on the old *Tonight* show when Johny Carson hosted it. Kamen talked of a time years before when he was living in New York and went for a meal to the Stage Delicatessen in downtown Manhattan. People go there after a show, and the waiters are known for their wit and occasional rudeness. On one particularly hot and humid day while Milt Kamen was eating his meal his waiter was called over to a man who complained about the terrible heat. The man demanded that the air conditioning be turned on. "Okay, sir," the waiter answered. "We shall turn on the air conditioning." A few minutes later, the man called the waiter over again: "It's really cold and drafty now," he said. "Please turn the air conditioning off!" "It will be done right away," Kamen's waiter replied.

It was not too long until the man demanded the air conditioning be turned on again. The same cycle went on and on for half an hour.

When Milt Kamen could not take it any longer, he said to the waiter: "My God! On again, off again. He must be driving you waiters crazy."

The waiter turned to him and said, "He's not driving us crazy. You see, we have no air conditioning here."

You might ask what this story has to do with my reading in Rochester and I must confess that there is little connection. But Ken must have liked it well enough to repeat the story to some friends we visited that night. The following Sunday we had a very nice audience at the Jewish Community Center. Many in attendance were of Polish-Jewish descent. They never grew up in German culture, never went through the terrible experiences of the extermination camps, and were unable to understand why I didn't show any bitterness toward the new Germany. They didn't understand why many German Jews visited Germany after the war. I explained that one cannot hold the new generation responsible for what their parents and grandparents had done. Many Jews have gone back for visits to Germany, especially at the invitation of the new German government. The hatred cannot go on and on. We also know that quite a few non-Jews saved Jews by risking their own lives in those terrible years of Nazi rule in Germany, Poland, and other occupied European countries.

I had gone to Rochester by train, but Joan; husband, Mel; and the grandchildren arrived at the lecture by car. Afterwards, we rode home to Syracuse together.

What a coincidence it was, not long thereafter, to be watching the Health News on a local TV station and to see the only son of Ken and Paula Walton talk about his medical research. Dr. Ralph Walton, a psychiatrist in Youngstown, Ohio, was concerned that the newly developed artificial sweetener Aspertame, sold under the trade name Nutrasweet, might provoke certain kinds of psychiatric reactions. He warned against the consumption of certain diet drinks containing the sweetener. The manufacturer had its own experts available to allay any concerns the public might have about the product. About two weeks later I saw Dr. Walton on a nationally televised interview. He was to write many articles for medical journals in the United States and England.

♣   ♣   ♣

In October of 1988, again through arrangements made by Ms. Trudy Garfunkel, I was interviewed by WEVD, one of the oldest New York City radio stations. Ruth Jacobs was the interviewer. In answer to her question about how I kept my religious views and my medical objectivity separate, I replied that medicine and my Jewish heritage have always gone together. I never neglected my Jewish heritage.

Ms. Jacobs also asked what inspired me to write my book, whereupon I replied: "I felt compelled to write because I did not see any autobiography by any of the other immigrant doctors, and, besides, I had to let people know and to unburden myself. I had to let people know what I did and how I had to see for myself if I could have done anything differently—if it was all worthwhile."

My search continues now, even in the present volume.

2

Michael, Our Special Child

I have not talked much about my disabled son, Michael, who is past the age of forty now. When he was barely five months old he had a devastating reaction to a Triple Vaccination immunization to inoculate against Diptheria, Pertusis, and Tetanus (D.P.T.). This resulted in severe seizures that rendered him mentally retarded and physically disabled. He is a quadriplegic and has been unable to speak clearly. A reaction to one of his seizure medications resulted in chronic gingivitis years ago, which led to the loss of all of his teeth.

Since the beginning of his illness, Michael has suffered from frequent convulsive seizures. Yet, through it all, he remains able to express himself. And when he smiles at us or our friends, or tries to hug us, he makes our day very special. When you are the parent of a disabled child or adult, you try to find meaning in a smile, a glance, a gesture.

Since Michael's early childhood I have been touched by a poem I thought had been composed by an anonymous writer. In May of 1978, I noticed in an Ann Landers column a request by a Mrs. Massimilla to reprint "her" poem. Mrs. Massimilla's husband is a pastor of a United Methodist Church in Delaware, and they have a severely retarded daughter. The title of the poem is:

Heaven's Very Special Child

A meeting was held quite far from Earth!
It's time again for another birth.
Said the angels to the Lord above,
This special Child will need much love.
His progress may be slow,
Accomplishment he may not show.
And he'll require extra care
From the folks he meets down there.
He may not run or laugh or play,
His thoughts may seem quite far away.
In many ways he won't adapt,
And he'll be known as handicapped.
So let's be careful where he's sent.
We want his life to be content.
Please, Lord, find the parents who
Will do a special job for You.
They will not realize right away
The leading role they're asked to play.
But with this child sent from above
Comes stronger faith and richer love.
And soon they'll know the privilege given
In caring for their gift from Heaven.
Their precious charge so meek and mild
Is Heaven's Very Special Child.

Some of my secular friends will probably tell me that they don't believe in the Lord and angels, but any poem or story that can move some people to tears and gives many thousands hope is true in a deeper sense.

It was the seizure problem that caused Herta and me to take Michael in the early sixties for neurological diagnosis and therapeutic evaluation at New York's Columbia Presbyterian Center. He was started there on Dilantin, one of the oldest anti-epileptic drugs, and with the help of this medication the number of seizures Michael experienced diminished. At one time, when the convulsions again got more out of control, Dr. Wright of the Upstate Medical Center added Mysoline to the Dilantin. This combination freed Michael from seizures for about a month, but soon they returned. Michael was kept on this combination while Dr. John K. Wolf, professor of neurology at our Syracuse Medical Center, tried to determine through blood tests the most effective dosage of the drugs. When in the late seventies Dr. Wolf took a year's sabbatical to do research on a new book, he felt that I could handle Michael quite well during his absence. If any questions arose, I could contact his colleague Dr. James Yurdin, another member of the neurological staff.

Dr. Yurdin adjusted the dosages of Dilantin and Mysoline from time to time, but Michael's seizures were still not controlled. Dr. Yurdin tried one of the newer drugs called Depakote. Unfortunately, Michael showed no improvement, and the side effects were rather severe. Gradually, the Depakote was discontinued and he was back on his old medication again. We never regretted our experiment with Depakote. If we hadn't tried it we would have thought that we had missed out on another opportunity to help our son.

At that time, Dr. Yurdin made me aware of the fact that (after his many years in practice) he wanted to get away from emergency medicine, especially seizure disorders. He recommended that we consult one of his younger colleagues, who specialized in the treatment of convulsions. Dr. Yurdin was kind enough to transfer all of Michael's records to his new neurologist, Dr. Nabil Aziz.

Dr. Aziz, who has treated Michael for the past several years, started our son on Tegretol, a medication that had helped many of my relatives and friends over the years. As always, Michael became seizure free for about two weeks, and then the old pattern of seizures returned: two mild convulsions every few days. If the medication levels in his blood became high or above normal, that often lead to even more seizures, or it could make him more hyperactive, which would cause tremors and involuntary movements. Dr. Aziz, as I remember, placed Michael on an additional drug named Tranzene.

I took care of Michael's medical problems with the help of my own internist, Dr. Paul Kronenberg. In the spring and summer Michael was allergic to pollen, and around Labor Day the ragweed season would begin. If he also developed a cold his bronchial tubes would become congested and I would have to start him on an antibiotic. Whenever Michael would have a fever, Eleene Seeber, our helper for more than three decades, would stay with him during the night, checking on his temperature. We would administer Tylenol whenever his temperature rose above 101 degrees during the night. If nausea or vomiting developed, we would treat it with a Tigan suppository.

I recall vividly the time when Michael was not completely controlled, but had mostly minor seizures. He was on Tegretol. Maureen Green, a local TV personality, had spoken at our neighborhood Soule Library on "A Day in the Life of an Anchor Woman in the 1990s." It had been just a few years earlier, in 1987, soon after my autobiography came out, that Maureen aired on her news broadcast an interview with me at my office at the State Tower Building. A large portion of the segment was about my book. Around the same time, I appeared on the Selma Radin show, called "Jewish Journal." I have wonderful tapes of both of these programs.

Ms. Green's talk at Soule Library was a result of the loss of her job at CBS, just around the time of the birth of her youngest child, when she was unable to work as many hours as management expected of her. The whole community seemed to be in an uproar: the mayor sent her a beautiful letter urging her to stay in Syracuse. Both the local NBC and ABC stations offered her anchor jobs. She had worked at the ABC station before, and Carrie Lazarus, an anchor woman, had been Maureen's close friend for many years. So, Maureen was once again working at ABC's Channel 9.

Ms. Green remembered her TV broadcast about my book in 1987, and I gave her an autographed copy at the time of her talk at the library. Joan took the most wonderful pictures of us on that occasion. Soon thereafter, Ms. Green invited us to watch her five o'clock news broadcast "live" from the studio, with the help of a very kind and knowledgeable TV engineer.

Michael had quite a few pictures from Maureen, and he saw her on TV every day. The whole family was very happy when she wanted to pay him a visit on his birthday, November 9. He had a busy and happy day, seeing visitors and receiving phone calls. But, shortly before the end of Maureen Green's news broadcast, Michael had a seizure. We had to put him to bed and he was soon fast asleep. The stress of the seizures can be quite draining.

I was going to cancel the newscaster's visit, but both Joan and Eleene begged me not to. Michael had looked forward to her visit all day. So, when she came at the expected time, we talked in a low voice while Michael slept. Suddenly, he opened his eyes, his face beaming to see Ms. Green. He gave Maureen a big hug and put her hand toward his face, a sign that he liked her. We took some of the best pictures ever that day.

Michael, of course, continued to watch the ABC local news. When he was admitted to Crouse Irving Memorial Hospital for the first time in about twenty-five years, he saw Maureen at five o'clock on the TV in his room. There was no doubt in his eyes that he was visiting with an old friend and it made him feel at home.

Michael was admitted to the hospital on this particular occasion because even the usually quite effective Tegretol, combined with Tranxene, did not eliminate his seizures. At the time, three drugs imported from Europe had been approved by the U.S. Food and Drug Administration. Dr. Aziz put Michael on one named Felbatol, which was receiving glowing reports in many popular magazines. It seemed to work well in the beginning—like all the new anticonvulsants—but gradually Michael started to gag and was unable to keep food or medications down. Dr. Kronenberg came to the house and agreed that Michael should be hospitalized under Dr. Aziz's care. Since he was somewhat dehydrated, Michael was also placed on intravenous fluids and he was gradually weaned from the Felbatol.

When Michael's Felbatol was gradually discontinued, Dr. Aziz started him on one of the other new European drugs—this one under the trade name Neurontin. Unfortunately, Michael suffered the same ill effects from the new drug as he had with the Felbatol. He was gagging and unable to swallow. Intravenous tubes had to be used to feed and hydrate him while the Neurotin was gradually withdrawn. I believe that Dr. Ramachandran attended Michael neurologically at this time, while Dr. Aziz had to be out of town. Eventually Michael was put on the old and proven standby Dilantin, while he was still on Tegretol.

But Michael had yet another major hurdle to overcome. Whenever his blood levels of Tegretol or Dilantin were in the above normal range, he would become hyperactive and start to shake. To counteract this hyperactivity, he was placed on Klonopin, another anticonvulsant that he had never been on before. Sadly, Michael experienced several seizures every day, mostly of the more severe grand mal type. It was found that the frequency and severity of the seizures was a reaction to Klonopin, which was soon discontinued with good results. At the end of his hospital stay, Michael was back on Dilantin and Phenobarbital.

Michael experienced one of the most trying times of his life during that three-month period at Crouse Irving Memorial, and we are grateful to Rabbi Ezring of Temple Concord, who saw him every week, and to Rabbi Sherman, who came with Cantor Pearlman. Both would try to get a smile out of Michael when he didn't feel much like smiling. Even Rabbi Yakov Rapoport, of the Orthodox Lubavitch Movement, brought Michael some Sabbath flowers and placed a pray card on his bedside.

At the time of his hospital admission I decided that Michael would have to go to a nursing facility after his discharge. In spite of all the good care the home aides were giving him, Michael needed round-the-clock specialized nursing care that only such a facility could provide. Frequently some of the home aides would become sick or would call in with an emergency of their own. A substitute had to come in, a person who didn't know Michael's case. In addition, I recalled that two or three years earlier Dr. Yurdin had told me that I was getting too old to take care of Michael twenty-four-hours-a-day. I wasn't ready to admit that I couldn't handle my son's care, but I was ready now. When Michael was finally medically ready to be discharged from the hospital, he had to wait until a bed became available for him at the Jewish Home of Central New York, located just a few minutes from our house. Our friend Eleene Seeber, who cared for Michael in our home for three decades now stays with him in his new surroundings night and day. She cooperates fully with the aides and nurses to give him the best care possible.

In the beginning she stayed with Michael overnight in our house, sleeping in a reclining chair in Michael's room. Soon she realized that she needed to go home and sleep in her own bed and take care of herself as well.

At the Jewish Home Michael is under the able care of Dr. A. Albert Tripodi and his staff. Michael's blood levels of his antiseizure drugs and for other medications are taken at the home. If there is any difficulty, Dr. Tripodi gets in touch with Dr. Aziz, Michael's neurologist, who also receives all the laboratory reports. Eleene, by the way, also stays at the home all the time.

It was clear from the start how well Michael was taken care of by the Jewish Home's friendly and dedicated nurses and staff. The Social Service Department, the activities directors, and others are always tremendously helpful to relatives of the residents. The patients, who come from all the various denominations, are kind to each other and often fun to watch. They are on healthy and satisfying diets and receive good, nutritious meals. In favorable weather the patients are encouraged to get out of doors and walk around or be wheeled around the spacious grounds.

Michael has television in his room or he can see cable programs on large sets in the hall or in TV rooms in other parts of the building. Michael enjoys his various programs, many of which include dancing, singing, piano or guitar playing, and even funny sketches. With the help of an aide or a nurse, Michael is able to sit outside under a large umbrella or to be wheeled around to visit with other residents. There are lots of activities for him as well: singing, piano-playing, guitar performances, special lectures and comedy shows. For many years— at least until more recently—my sister-in-law, Lucy van der Linde, now over ninety, would come each year from California to visit us in Syracuse. She never failed to visit the Jewish Home and to entertain the residents with a piano recital.

I am so very grateful for the comprehensive medical care Michael receives at the Jewish Home from Dr. A. Albert Tripodi, who is assisted by his able nurse practitioner, Christine Heagle Bahn. Michael's convulsions are for the most part controlled by Dilantin and Phenobarbital, the first medications he was ever prescribed. The medication levels are checked regularly: blood is drawn right at the home and Dr. Tripodi Sr., either reduces or increases the dosage after lab reports are reviewed. If any special neurological problems arise, Dr. Aziz is contacted. The other two attending physicians at the home, Dr. Tripodi Jr., and Dr. Steven K. Alexander, treat Michael along the same lines. With this kind of skillful care, I don't have anything to worry about.

3

Retired But Not Forgotten

Reporting on Michael's ailments would be enough for an entire book all its own. But my life is filled with many experiences. Though I am retired and no longer practice medicine, some of my former patients still seek my general medical advice. In the earlier years of retirement, before my own health worsened, I felt well enough at my age to pay a visit to some sick, elderly people in the hope of spending a few hours with them, thereby giving their spouses/family caregivers a bit of a breather to enable them to get away for a little while. These short respites are vital to all caregivers. Time away from the stress of their loved one's situation, even if only for a few hours, helps to recharge the emotional and physical batteries. Occasionally, I would receive some requests for visits through Temple Concord's Caring Coalition, under the able leadership of Celia Block. At other times patients would call me directly.

I remember Celia Block so well. She was a retired Sunday school teacher from Utica, New York, who had written a small volume, a story for young children, set to music and richly illustrated. *When Sabbath Came He Rested* describes each day of creation. Celia Block had a host of ailments, and she was practically blind. I had given her a copy of my *Once a Doctor,* and she was not quite sure if she could empathize with it, coming from a different background. Besides, she had nobody who would have the time to read the book to her. I visited her on about eight occasions to read from my autobiography and to discuss it with her. She enjoyed our visits and we both looked forward to the next one. I was very happy to be a source of enjoyment and a few moments of pleasure for her. When Celia Block passed away in 1992, I was invited to the memorial service at Syracuse Temple Beth-El with my daughter, Joan. There we met Celia's daughter, Margie Levine and her husband, as well as various other relatives. We also met again Ms. Bonnie, her reliable help at home during the many years of her illness.

A few years ago, I was able to see at his home Professor Stephen M. Baron, a resident of Syracuse who is a professor of political science and history at Oswego State University. (I still have a 1982 article he wrote for the *Syracuse Sunday Herald.*) He was diagnosed with Multiple Sclerosis (MS) at the Dr. Mary Walker Clinic at Oswego and sent for further medical evaluation to the Upstate Medical Center in Albany, where he was examined and treated by the neurological resident, Dr. Nancy Havernick. Like something out of a movie script, they fell in love and decided to get married. "Not everyone gets to marry his doctor," Baron remarked. He is a native of Boston, while Dr. Havernick hails form Minneapolis.

Rabbi Moshe Adler came from Minneapolis to perform the marriage ceremony, and so did Dr. Havernick's parents. Professor Baron's friends, who were in teaching positions with him in Illinois, Maryland, and Virginia, were also invited. The couple wanted to share this joyful occasion with as many people as possible. They selected the Jewish Home, where residents and staff joined them at the ceremony. I believe they have two daughters now, two years apart in age, who celebrate the same birthdate!

I remember that in 1983 an article appeared in *Commentary* magazine titled "Living Without Health," and two months later, among several responses, there appeared a reply by Professor Baron, with a fine discussion of his struggle with MS. In 1988, a few years later, he wrote a fine piece in the *Syracuse Jewish Observer* titled "Don't Believe It! People Still Care." During the past few years, as his disease progressed, he had to rely on forearm crutches or a wheelchair. From time to time he fell, blaming his own "clumsiness." But there was never a time when somebody didn't try to help him. For quite some time now, Professor Baron has been president of the Orthodox Synagogue "Young Israel Shaarei Torah" of Syracuse. I am very happy that he enjoyed my book.

4

The Doctor Is Hangin' in There!

At this point it might be advisable to write a bit about my own health, so that no one will have reason to criticize me this time for talking mostly about other people and not enough about myself.

The first hint that I had any kind of heart problem came, as I recall, with a fast pulse and a palpitation during my last years of high school in Breslau, Germany. It was before the actual Nazi era, but threatening signs were on the political horizon. This palpitation was also the reason that I never became an outstanding swimmer. (Several years ago, I took some special classes at my local YMCA under the guidance of a young instructor named Fran Gamber. One of the other pupils, a woman older than myself, seemed a little jealous. She must have thought that I mastered the survival technique of floating better than she did. She didn't have to be jealous; I wasn't all that good.)

It is strange that similar experiences reported by the philosopher Mortimar Adler about how his nonparticipation in swimming and other physical activities almost destroyed his professional career made me interested in his writings. He wrote his autobiography *Philosopher at Large* when he was eighty and continued his reflections in another book titled *A Second Look in the Rearview Mirror* when he was ninety years of age.

My own medical story is, of course, quite a different one. In addition to the many years of experiencing palpitations, heart pounding, and similar complaints, I have had high blood pressure (hypertension) for several decades. I was treated in New York state by Dr. Fred Hiss, who died in his nineties quite a few years ago. He was succeeded by Dr. Murray Grossman, who was occasionally replaced by Dr. David Nash. After Grossman's retirement, I placed myself under the care of Dr. Paul Kronenberg.

From the start the primary drugs used in the treatment of my hypertension have been diuretics. I was put on Hydrodiuril, Renese, and Renese-R. Unfortunately, they all have one side effect called hypokalemia. In other words, my potassium level would become quite low, coupled with electrocardiographic changes. Even the administration of Slow-K, a drug helpful in relieving the hypokalemia, was not successful. Soon I developed quite a bothersome arrhythmia with premature ventricular contractions (PVCs). At that time I was put on Tenormin, another antihypertensive drug, which regulated my arrhythmia quite well. Aside from the side effect of experiencing cold extremities, the slow pulse rate caused by the Tenormin bothered me quite a bit. The Tenormin was gradually discontinued.

After the older diuretics had caused my potassium deficiency, with all its complications, I was started on a newer diuretic called Dyazide, which contained a potassium-sparing agent. I am still taking one Dyazide capsule each day. In addition I am taking 10 mg of Vasotec for my hypertension. To prevent me from having a heart attack or stroke, Dr. Kronenberg has me take one children's aspirin each day as well. I am on a low-cholesterol diet, so I don't require drug treatment to maintain my cholesterol level.

I still have heart palpitations and some shortness of breath, more so in the last two to three years. This forces me to stop occasionally while I am walking to take a brief rest. These symptoms might come on even at rest, while thinking of my responsibilities and the lack of time to perform all my duties. So, the prescription for Miltown or Meprobamate has helped me over the years. This mild tranquilizer also helps me to achieve uninterrupted sleep, whenever a problem arises during the night.

Actually, the older a person gets, the less sleep he or she needs. In thinking of the need for sleep, I am reminded of Dr. Ernest Sarason, a well-known surgeon, who several years ago was honored by the Syracuse Area Interreligious Council at a large dinner at Hotel Syracuse, attended by (at least) a thousand people. Not only was he honored for his part in interreligious understanding, but for fundraising on behalf of hospitals and for medicine in general, and Jewish charities. As was brought out at this large dinner gathering , Dr. Sarason was always fond of convertibles and drove them with the top up or down, depending on the season. When asked how he was able to run such a busy surgical practice, take care of his charity work, and still maintain a social life with his friends, his answer was that he always got along on five hours of sleep per day.

&   &   &

It was in 1989, when members of my family began offering me large glasses of water at all hours of the day. They had apparently read articles, written by laypeople in the general press, that every person should drink eight glasses of water every day. I didn't pay much attention until I found a large essay in *Parade* magazine written by the director of a sports institute. He suggested that his readers drink thirteen glasses of water each day. And it had to be water! All the juices people were drinking, all the fruits they ate, didn't count. Millions of people all over the world would excrete this excessive fluid intake anyway. And how could he recommend this excessive amount of water to people with edema (swelling) of the legs and ankles due to heart or kidney failure? Dr. Kronenberg agreed with me. There was also a speaker named Dr. Steven Scheinman at Upstate Medical Grand Rounds who talked about "Diuretics and Hyponatremia," a condition of salt or sodium loss in the blood. He mentioned polydipsia, the excessive drinking of fluid, as one cause of it. In the discussion I asked him about the article by the director of the sports institute in *Parade* magazine. He was very interested in this and similar articles, but had never seen any. The laypeople write for the lay press, and doctors write for other doctors. I wrote to two nationally known medical journals asking them to publish my letter regarding the excessive water intake. Both publications felt that there would not be enough interest among their respective readers, or that some doctors might reply who really were not sufficiently knowledgeable. I was amazed. How could major medical journals write long essays and editorials about diseases physicians hardly even encounter in their practices, while devoting no space to matters of immediate concern? Years ago I had sent letters to the "Letters to the Editor" column of very informative medical magazines, publications that were sent to the doctors free of charge—such as *Modern Medicine* or *Medical Tribune*. My letters were always printed. Now, since I am retired, they don't send these publications to me anymore. In retrospect, I don't regret that, as I am about one or two years behind in the reading of most journals to which I do subscribe.

        🐜   🐜   🐜

For years I had keratosis-lesions on my forehead, treated at first by dermatologist Dr. Harry Levitt, now retired. These skin lesions were never found to be malignant. In recent years I have been seen by Dr. Alfred Falcone, plastic surgeon, who sometimes excises or cauterizes the lesions, but mostly I can prevent the keratosis by using topical lotions to ease the dry skin. It was also Dr. Falcone who referred me to a podiatrist named Dr. Harold Rubinstein to relieve the callus formations on the soles of both my feet. There was also some fungus infection of my toenails, which was successfully treated. The callus formations were due to my low-fat-low-cholesterol diet. Over-the-counter arch supports are of considerable help here, and I don't have to see the podiatrist anymore unless new problems arise.

        🐒   🐒   🐒

Usually I see my ophthalmologist Dr. Anthony La Tessa about once a year. It is somewhat longer now since the family has taken over my 1991 automobile for college, household chores, and errands to the bank and post office. But gradually we catch up on all our medical appointments. At the time of my previous eye consultation, my eyeglass prescription was changed for the first time in my life. I was fitted with photogrey lenses now that I am very sensitive to bright sunlight.

        🐒   🐒   🐒

While Michael's medical situation has improved, mine has not. For about the past two or three years, I continued to experience palpitations and some shortness of breath whenever I had to hurry to catch an appointment. When these attacks occurred more frequently—even at rest—I was sent by Dr. Kronenberg to the cardiology group of Dr. William Berkery for an echocardiogram with a stress test. Dr. Anis Obeid, who had started this well-known cardiology group years ago, met with Dr. Berkery to interpret my x-rays and their electrocardiogram results. They seemed disturbed that the cardiac images showed a definite blockage of some coronary arteries. My results on the treadmill stress test were not too good either. When I became shortwinded, they put me on stretcher. They asked if I had ever taken Nitroglycerin, and when I told them no, they put a very mild tablet of the medication under my tongue. Soon the discomfort subsided.

After the procedure was completed, I was wheeled back to

Dr. Kronenberg's office. He had already been informed of the test findings by Dr. Berkery. Dr. Kronenberg placed me on Isordil (20 mg three times per day) as a preventive measure, and he prescribed Nitroglycerin sublingual tablets (1/200 gr) in case of an attack. Then Dr. Kronenberg sent me to Dr. Joseph Battaglia, another member of the cardiology group, who decided to do a heart catheterization to explore my coronary arteries. He could tell me then if I could be treated with drugs or if I needed the more invasive procedure known as angioplasty (the method of clearing blood vessels by inserting a balloon into an artery, inflating it, and then expanding the area through which the blood can flow). Not only could he open the coronary arteries with a balloon-type instrument, but he could also re- move any clot or thrombosis with a scissor-like instrument.

Dr. Battaglia performed the heart catheterization on December 16, 1994. He inserted the catheter into my right arm, as originally planned, and watched the moving pictures of my heart. Our chat during the procedure helped ease the tension. (He finally told me that I was a good patient and that I should write about this in my next book.)

I asked Dr. Battaglia what the angiogram indicated about the state of my coronary arteries. He told me that three major arteries were narrowed (stenotic) and filled with thrombotic plaques. An angioplasty, he said, would not be the answer. Instead, a triple bypass was recommended.

Before this diagnosis could sink in I was immediately wheeled back to my room by a male aide. He took me full speed, racing down the halls and up the elevator. Since early childhood I had been subject to motion sickness and this time was no exception. I was given ginger ale to relieve the symp- toms, but to no avail. Finally, after eating a little lunch the nausea subsided. I had been admitted with the understanding that I could stay overnight, but with the permission of Dr. Battaglia I left Crouse Irving Hospital the same evening. I appreciated very much his willingness to increase the dosage of my Isordil from 20 to 40 mg (one tablet three times a day).

I went back to Dr. Kronenberg to discuss Dr. Battaglia's

results. Rather than remain with Dr. Battaglia I chose to see Dr. Fred Parker, who had started the cardiac surgical unit at our Upstate Medical Center years ago and has trained numerous surgeons at that center as well as at other units at Syracuse's St. Joseph Hospital. Dr. Parker explained with great patience that a massive heart attack might occur if the bypass surgery was not performed. He stated that 90 percent of the successful cardiac operations cured the problem completely. Of the 10 percent that failed, those who did not die during the operation might suffer from a severe stroke, respiratory failure, or confusion. He promised to do the surgery himself, rather than assigning it to one of his assistants.

Although I had great confidence that I would recover well from bypass surgery, there was only one decision I could honestly make. I asked Dr. Parker if he would be angry with me if I didn't have the surgery. He laughed and replied that it was a free country and that he would not be at all offended. I also asked him to increase my Isordil dosage from one 40 mg tablet three times a day to one 40 mg tablet four times a day. This way I didn't have such a long interval between doses, my condition felt more under control, and I didn't have to take the Nitroglycerin tablets to relieve chest pressure and shortness of breath. He agreed to increase the dosage. When I phoned him to tell him that since the increase in the Isordil I was feeling so much better, he wished me well and hoped that I would continue to do fine.

The decision not to have the triple bypass was the only decision I could make. I was writing this book at the time and I was the only one who could write it and pay full attention to what I wanted to say. As a man in my eighties, I could not afford to be laid up with the surgery and the recovery period not knowing if I could write afterward. I was able to write and it was important for me to express my life experiences. I must say that most people to whom I tell this do not understand. But I do, and that is all that matters.

      🐾   🐾   🐾

At the end of 1994, we had our usual New Year's Eve party, a get-together started by Herta many years ago. There was no alcohol but many snacks, grape juice, and fruit salad. Our good friend Dr. Baurice Laffer had just been released from the hospital with a heart ailment, and his wife, Helen, was under the care of an orthopedist. Our good friend Roz Sagar was there with her son, Michael, who had been a roommate of mine for many years since I went with the senior group of Temple Society of Concord to the Nevele's or Kutscher's. Celebrating with us for the first time was a friend of my granddaughter, Sarah, from Le Moyne College, who in her spare time works at WCNY, the educational television station. Ralph Golio, a custodian at the local Howard Johnson's motel, who has done repair work at our house for decades, picked up Eleene Seeber from the Jewish Home to spend the evening with us. There was also Shirley Small, the widow of our good friend Alan Small, who died so young and meant so much to so many people. In attendance as well was Rita Seligman, widow of our good friend Dr. Hans Seligman, who died after a long illness at such an early age. Rita, our friend for over fifty years, came with her companion, Heinz Rothschild, and brought me a little gift—a sign which Sarah hung for me in the basement where my desk and typewriter are. The sign read "A clean, uncluttered desk is the sign of a SICK MIND!" Rita was the friend who years ago had asked me how I could possibly find anything on my desk—the clutter was so incredible—and offered to clean the desk for me. I never invited her to my basement study again. Now, after all those years, I do extend the invitation occasionally—but not to clean!

Everyone at the New Year's Eve party knew about my recent medical history and wouldn't let me lift a finger. The following week when I attended the Friday night services at Temple Society of Concord, many of the congregants had read in one of the bulletins about my hospital stay. I assured them that I was feeling better since my medication level had been changed.

Not surprisingly, I had been reading about the problems of coronary artery disease. Many friends reminded me again that

I should read Dr. Dean Ornish's *Reversing Heart Disease: The Only System Scientifically Proven to Reverse Heart Attack without Drugs or Surgery* (1990), a book that had appeared on the *New York Times* bestseller list. It comes highly recommended by, among others, Dr. Bernie Siegel, author of *Love, Medicine, and Miracles* and other volumes.

Dr. Ornish became interested in the subject of coronary artery research when in 1977 he studied under the famed heart surgeon Dr. Michael DeBakey in Houston, Texas. Dr. Ornish assisted Dr. DeBakey when the latter would perform bypass surgery. The patients were considered cured but they would then continue their sedentary lifestyle as well as eating fatty food and other high-cholesterol items, smoking, and other activities that were unhealthy. Eventually their coronary blockage would return. In 1977, while in medical school, Dr. Ornish took a year off, with support by Dr. Antonio Gotto (chief of medicine) and conducted a study of reversed heart disease without surgery. The result was his book with numerous case histories of patients whose coronary artery disease was reversed without drugs or surgery. These cases were very convincing.

Joan suggested that I watch a Phil Donohue program on unnecessary surgery—a very important concern for all of us. Sometimes such programs can be very helpful in informing us about new medical procedures. The part of the program that was of most interest for us featured Professor K. Lance Gould, Division of Cardiology, at the University of Texas in Houston. He showed the audience one of his patients, a pleasant, sixty-seven-year-old man who, because of his angina, had a stress test, which he failed miserably (I know how he feels!). When a heart catheterization was suggested to him he refused, because he was afraid that this would ultimately lead to a bypass. Dr. Gould changed his diet, put him on cholesterol-lowering drugs, and made him change his lifestyle. The patient is free from angina now, and his coronary artery disease shows complete reversal in the so-called Pet scan, a noninvasive procedure taken on an outpatient basis at the University of Texas Medical School.

After seeing this program, Joan made a telephone call to Dr. Gould's office in Houston. Since the professor was on a speaking tour abroad, Joan talked with his nurse, Mary Jane Hess, R.N., who has been most helpful to us. I wanted material regarding the cardiologist's ideas about reversal of coronary artery disease. Upon receiving it, I found out from the bibliography and from nurse Hess that Dean Ornish and Dr. Gould have written various papers together. The main difference between them is the fact that Dr. Ornish does not use drugs in reversal treatment, while Dr. Gould prescribes, for example, cholesterol-lowering medication since he likes to keep the cholesterol and triglycerides much lower in his reversal patients than is considered normal in the general population.

Since we received the literature we requested, Dr. Gould's office has been in touch with the echocardiogram and heart catheterization laboratories of Crouse Irving Hospital here in Syracuse and all the reports and copies of my films and videotapes are in the cardiologists possession. Now that cardiologists can observe and monitor patients who live out of state, I hope that Dr. Gould will be in touch as soon as he has come to a conclusion about my case. At that point he would communicate with Dr. Paul Kronenberg, my internist. I saw Dr. Kronenberg not long ago and he continues to support me in my decision not to have bypass surgery and my desire to take cholesterol-lowering drugs. So far, my cholesterol level has dropped considerably because of my almost vegetarian diet. I am not on a cholesterol-lowering medication at the present time. I might change my mind, though, after hearing from Dr. Gould.

I asked Dr. Kronenberg if he felt I should see another cardiologist—someone who is more familiar with alternative methods of reversing coronary artery disease. He thought not: there would be no reason to invite more confusion with an abundance of opinions. Besides, having to start all over with another cardiologist would mean more tests, more office visits, and more frustration. I recall seeing studies in which a high percentage of people were prescribed treatment with hypertensive drugs for high blood pressure when in fact their pressure seemed quite normal outside the doctor's office.

         🐜   🐜   🐜

Though my health was a bit uncertain at the time, on a positive note, there had been a great many expressions of love and concern from all my relatives and friends. These messages still come in daily. I received warm and loving letters from my ninety-year-old sister-in-law, Lucy, who lives in Sunnyvale, California, and from my ninety-year-old former patient Florence Bonner, as well as my ninety-year-old cousin Anna Spitz from Detroit. All were worried about me when they heard of my condition. Dorothy Lehrer, an elderly former patient with whom I share a birthdate, never forgets to communicate with me, offering advice and comfort from the experiences she has had with other family members who also suffer with coronary artery disease. My cousins Eric and Inge Spitz, from Toronto, talk with me weekly on the telephone to learn about my progress. Eric had a bypass operation quite a few years ago, and he remains on medication—the type I am taking now. Inge never forgets to report my progress to Eric's sister, Uschi, and her husband, Johnny.

Among our friends for many years, Roz Sagar has been helpful during my illness as has Rita Seligman and Linda Cantor, whose father, Irving, had bypass surgery but must still take a good bit of medication. Linda Ehrich, a former supervising nurse when our Michael was still managed by home aides, has been a great comfort to my daughter, Joan. Linda's father also suffers from a cardiac condition. Our friend Paul Bloomfield is in constant telephone touch with us, and Rabbi Ezring of the Temple Society Concord—a man with considerable illness in his own family—still takes time out to visit Michael and to check up on me. I also received a wonderful call from our good friend Natalie Kalette, who had read about my illness in one of the synagogue's bulletins. Her husband, Hank, had to undergo open-heart surgery some time ago.

We continue to receive a great many calls and letters from

well-meaning people who cannot contribute very much to a discussion of my physical and emotional well-being. Nevertheless, we certainly appreciate their interest, their concern, and their good wishes. During this time, I hardly ever communicated with people over the telephone. I was occupied at my typewriter in my study, surrounded by my library. Unlike my grandchildren, I don't understand anything about computers. Joan and the grandchildren are my telephone answering service.

For a while I had trouble reaching the rest of the family upstairs while I was working. When I needed something I would knock on the floor with a ruler to get their attention, but this technique only works if they are in certain areas of the house where the knocking can be heard. But our friend Eleene found a fabulous solution. She presented me with a wireless intercom system, one which allows one receiver to be near me while two other units are upstairs. The family and I have perfect communication now.

         🐜   🐜   🐜

There was a call both Joan and I had to make not long ago, soon after the diagnosis of my coronary artery disease. We made the call to our cousin Dr. Werner Spitz, a forensic pathologist in Detroit, and his wife, Anne. We didn't know of his existence until 1990. At that time, I believe, Johnny Miller, our cousin in Toronto, saw him on television when Werner was called as a coroner to the scene of a serious accident in nearby Canada. Johnny's call to Detroit located this long-lost cousin.

I remember that Werner's father, Dr. Siegfried Spitz, who had practiced medicine in Germany, was practicing in the German town of Stargard. He saw what was coming for the Jews and decided in 1933 to leave Germany to emigrate to Palestine. Before he and his wife, Anna, packed their belongings and left the country, Siegfried visited his parents and grandmother and grandfather, who lived in Breslau (now Wroclaw). I was about twenty years old and studying to be a physician. My cousin left me some of his medical books to study. Back in Stargard, Siegfried and Anna picked up their belongings, their seven-year-old son, and left the country.

When I left Nazi Germany in 1939, I never knew if they were alive and well or exactly where they were until we received that surprising and happy message from Johnny Miller in Toronto.

Until 1948, when the Jewish state was declared, Dr. Spitz risked his life every day, seeing Arab patients in far away villages, always accompanied by Anna. He was never afraid. "Nothing is more precious than a human life," he used to say. After the Jewish state was established, he practiced medicine among the Jewish population until he decided to return to Germany in 1956. There he opened an office in Frankfurt and practiced medicine until his retirement in 1970.

While in Germany, Anna went to medical school and received her degree, as did her daughter Karnie, born after their emigration to Palestine. Their daughter is now Dr. Karnie Frank of Bloomfield, Michigan, with her husband (also a doctor) and their wonderful family. In 1976, Dr. Siegfried and Anna Spitz moved to the United States and have stayed at the home of their daughter and son-in-law.

When I got in touch with Werner and Anne Spitz first in 1990, his father was quite ill and had to be hospitalized. There Dr. Siegfried Spitz died of pneumonia at the age of ninety-five. "I always knew I would be a doctor," said Werner, "because of my parents. I cannot imagine life without Father. Even when you know he is older, losing him cannot be described. It is the saddest day of my life."

As a professor of forensic pathology, Werner Spitz lectures in the United States and in Canada as well as in Israel. He is the author of *Medico-legal Investigation of Death.* He worked for seven years at the coroner's office in Israel and saw a single murder case during that whole time. He went to Baltimore, Maryland, for further training and met his wife to be. Anne came from England and was a nurse. When they married, Werner decided to emigrate to the United States. But,

according to the U.S. immigration law, it was required that he
return to the country of his birth (Germany) and stay there for
two years before petitioning for a visa. Werner hadn't been to
Germany since he was seven years old. In a speech he gave at
his daughter Rhona's wedding, Werner explained that Rhona
was born in Germany and she was eleven months old when
they came to the United States. Rhona's two brothers are doctors now.

This just goes to show how even an illness can have its
positive side. I might never have known about these long-lost
relatives had someone not mentioned them when inquiring
about my health.

Dr. K. Lance Gould, the consulting cardiologist in Houston,
received my films, cassettes, and reports from various physicians and from the echocardiograms and heart catheterization
laboratories. He sent me an outline of his coronary artery
reversal program. Dr. Gould indicated in his letter to me that I
should be on a low-fat, low-carbohydrate, high-protein diet. In
spite of the fact that my weight has been fairly normal for
quite some time, Dr. Gould recommended that I lose seven
pounds. He instructed me about exercise and prescribed Zocor
for me. It is a cholesterol-lowering drug. He intended to bring
my total cholesterol down to below 140 mg. In addition, he
prescribed Norvasc (5 mg daily) along with my usual Isordil
dosage to help the angina, and I could continue my daily children's aspirin.

For the next three months laboratory tests were performed
to check cholesterol, triglycerides, and liver function. Thereafter, the tests would be taken every four months. Dr. Gould
also recommended that I take high daily doses of beta
carotene, vitamin E, and vitamin C. He keeps in constant contact with Dr. Kronenberg.

5

I Still Have an Opinion or Two on Medicine

I still attend lectures at my neighborhood Soule Library when invited. The "Midday Medleys," usually arranged by librarian Liz DeMarco, take place once a week during the noon hour. She loves to invite as a speaker the well-known and controversial psychiatrist Dr. Thomas S. Szasz, because she will be assured of a large audience. Dr. Szasz's influential book *The Myth of Mental Illness* appeared in 1961, and he has written many books since then. As I remember, he considers most psychiatrists "jailers," whose patients suffer as much from them as "the Jews did under the Nazis." Psychiatric consultation should only be on a voluntary basis, but no psychiatrist has the right to hospitalize a patient against that person's will. But how many patients with delusions or hallucinations, some with the urge to do harm to others or themselves, would voluntarily wish to go to a hospital for their emotional problems?

Years ago, whenever a patient who tried to commit suicide was admitted to a general hospital, that person was automatically transferred to a psychiatric unit for observation. Not anymore. As Dr. Szasz maintains, in a free society everybody has the right to commit suicide, and we should not interfere. Yet I

53

have seen numerous letters from people who tried to end their lives more than once. In these letters they often express gratitude to their psychiatrist for showing them the value and beauty of life.

At one of his Soule Library lectures, Szasz told us that patients often ask him, as the doctor, if he is religious. They have a right to ask, and he always gives them his standard answer: "I have no religious bone in my body." But by saying that he excludes a huge number of patients from treatment, since a high percentage of the population admits to having some kind of religious outlook. As Robert Coles, the well-known psychiatrist and writer, tells us in his *Spiritual Life of Children,* he interviewed youngsters from all over the world—children of Jewish, Christian, Muslim, agnostic, and atheistic backgrounds—and, strange as it seems, all of these children had quite similar ideas of God, the afterlife, and the meaning of life on this earth. Even Suzy Szasz, the daughter of Dr. Szasz, who describes in her own fine book, *Living with It,* her battle with the systemic affliction known as Lupus Erythematosus, states a position contrary to her famous father. In spite of her love for him, her views were more in tune with her Catholic friends (without being Catholic herself) than with her famous psychiatrist father.

Most doctors were justly critical of an article Dr. Szasz wrote nearly twenty years ago in *Medical Economics.* It was titled "Stop Poking Around in Your Patients' Lives!" In it he offers that a nonpsychiatrist should not give advice in non-physical matters. In her book his daughter tells us that her father checked closedly the treatment of any of her physicians and asked them to change therapies when warranted. Granted, he had a medical degree, but is it permissible for a psychiatrist (a nonpracticing medical doctor with a specific specialty in matters of the mind) to give advice to the internist or family physician, while the medical doctor is forbidden to talk about the psychological problems of his patient? It might surprise some to know that almost all the patients of a general practitioner or an internist have some psychological problems. In my professional experience, the biggest complaint patients have about their medical care is that doctors just don't take the time to sit down and talk with them. Those patients are not psychotic; they have no major psychiatric problems. But they like to know how to live with their illness, how to get along with their spouses, their in-laws, and their neighbors. They might even want to know what books to read. For decades now, medical college authorities have suggested that medical students take more courses in the humanities, and lately they have found some hope in a new trend. In some of the medical schools 50 percent of the graduates are women! According to some people who study the healthcare delivery system, women seem more compassionate to their patients and are willing to sit down and listen.

At one of his lectures, given at Soule Library in December of 1993, Dr. Szasz's topic was "Our Right to Drugs: The Case for a Free Market." The claim was made that in a free society drug use without prescription should be legal: there would be no black market in illegal drugs, and the addiction problem would be solved. I am no expert in this matter, but I cannot understand this "solution." Imprisonment may not be the answer, but forced treatment of addicts might be. Many addicts have become criminals who kill, rape, and wound their victims without remembering anything about it afterwards. Why should they have the right to buy drugs without restriction? They wouldn't know enough about the side effects, the dosage levels, the various available forms of the drug, or the precautions to be taken. All they are interested in is satisfying their cravings. No other citizens are able to purchase their medications for heart ailments, intestinal disease, or viruses without a proper prescription. And the drug users shouldn't either.

ꙮ   ꙮ   ꙮ

Why is there so much disagreement over physician-assisted suicide of the type advocated by Jack Kevorkian? As I have mentioned before, many of these suicidal patients suffer from depression and wouldn't want to commit suicide if they thought about it carefully. The famous editor of the *New York Times Book Review,* writer and Tolstoy biographer Anatole Broyard, left us a wonderful book titled *Intoxicated by My Illness.* It consists of a number of essays, written after he was stricken with prostate cancer in 1989. These essays were edited by his widow, Alexandra. Rather than becoming despondent, he made fine observations about himself and others, and considered the years since the diagnosis of his malignancy the most productive of his life.

Another reason for the wish to commit suicide is the failure of the physician to prescribe powerful pain medication when needed. One of the best features of the *Journal of the American Medical Association* is a column titled "A Piece of My Mind," where physicians share their most inspiring experiences. Some of the essays were reprinted in an anthology in 1988. One of the pieces, which appeared originally in 1987, was called "Painful Prescriptions." It told the stories of three people, all suffering from cancer. All three had received prescriptions from their own physicians for strong narcotic medications, but each had to move to another part of the country for retirement, or for other reasons. None of their new doctors were willing to give these advanced cancer patients the original narcotics, for fear that the patients would become "addicted." Some physicians used the lame excuse that they did not the have triplicate forms required by the state. All three terminal cancer patients became despondent, that is until they returned home to their original physicians, received the appropriate pain managing drugs, and found life worth living again.

A physician might err, of course, and issue a prescription for a narcotic or a tranquilizer to an addict. In *Once a Doctor* I told the story of the young woman who came to my office door asking for a strong tranquilizer. Her mother had just died and she had to get through the funeral. Not long after providing her with the prescription she requested, I found out that the mother was very much alive and feeling well.

6

Sharing My Stories
and Anecdotes

When I was in my seventies I had planned to semi-retire but I could not decrease my workload, what with office rents going up and malpractice insurance rates climbing. I finally did retire in September of 1987.

"What are you worried about?" my granddaughter, Sarah, asked me when I complained about lack of time. "Everybody likes to retire. Then you have nothing to do."

She forgets that I have a second calling, namely, my writing, which gives me immense satisfaction. By the way, after spending much of their lives in medicine, many prominent physicians who ordinarily would have pushed their sons and daughters into the medical profession don't feel bad at all if their children go into history, engineering, or some other area.

     🐾   🐾   🐾

Earlier, I discussed my grandson, Maurice's, review of my autobiography. Here I shall report on an analysis of *Once a Doctor* for a professor at Onondaga Community College

(OCC), the first college my granddaughter, Sarah Raichelson, attended after graduation from Jamesville Dewitt High School. Students were able to afford the tuition at OCC when the higher fees at other universities were well out of reach. While attending OCC, Sarah developed an interest in subjects which had never meant a lot to her before. In her younger years she gave up playing the piano soon after her lessons stopped. Yet now she sits down at the piano and plays notes from a melody she might have just heard in a musical performance. She also plays at the Passover Seder, where we sit at the table with our Jewish and non-Jewish friends to sing from the Haggadah in Hebrew or in English.

Sarah has remained in contact with some of her professors from OCC, especially Dr. Sandra Fiske, professor of psychology. It was Dr. Fiske who stimulated Sarah's interest in psychology, the subject she later majored in at Le Moyne College in Syracuse. From time to time Professor Fiske invites my granddaughter to present a project or exhibit to her class. The project or demonstration is often shared by Elise Shefrin, a friend and fellow student at Le Moyne. Elise and her sister, Amy, have been Sarah's friends for many years, and their father, Dr. Bruce Shefrin, is a professor of political science at Le Moyne.

Dr. Kathleen Forrest, professor of English at Onondaga Community College, evaluated a paper of Sarah's in 1992. The paper was titled "The Teaching Value of Folklore as Told by My Grandfather." Sarah's excellent mark was accompanied by the following comment: "An outstanding collection and analysis! Thanks for sharing it!" In preparation for her paper, I recall a period of four or five weeks in which Sarah taped our conversations; she would ask me to tell her stories from my book, recall tales and proverbs from Germany, recount my experiences once I had arrived in America, or recite tales from the Talmud.

☙   ☙   ☙

One story that received special praise concerned the two Jewish friends who happened to run into each other before Rosh Hashanah—the Jewish New Year holiday. The Jewish teaching tells us that sins committed against other human beings will only be forgiven by God if the offending person apologizes to the party offended. In line with this teaching, one of the friends said to the other: "You know, we have not been on good business terms together. I might have taken advantage of you. But Rosh Hashanah is coming up, so let's let bygones be bygones. Let us start a new life, and I wish everything that you wish for me." The other friend turned to him and said, "You see, now you start again!"

                                   ₳   ₳   ₳

I think that another story is worth repeating here: In this case two psychiatrists are talking to each other when a third one comes by and says "Hello. How are you?" The older one of the two says "I wonder what he means by that?"

                                     ₳   ₳   ₳

I shall, repeat here a story from *Once a Doctor* about Karl Lueger, mayor of Vienna, Austria, who gave the bad anti-Semitic speeches, full of hatred against Jews. When asked how he could say such a thing in spite of all his many Jewish friends, he answered, "I determine who is a Jew."

                                     ₳   ₳   ₳

There was another event reported by Sarah regarding a young mother who brought her two children to a pediatrician complaining that they didn't feel well. The pediatrician didn't find anything wrong with them, but the mother brought them back again and again. Finally, the doctor told the mother that she was making too much of a fuss about nothing and that she should consider seeing a psychiatrist for help. So the mother went to a psychiatrist and was not seen by the pediatrician for quite some time. When the doctor eventually met her on the street one day and asked "How are the children?" the mother answered, "Who cares?"

   🐜 🐜 🐜

Sometimes when Sarah and Maurice stay up late and don't awaken until late the next morning, I offer a German proverb that comes to mind: "Morgen, morgen, nur nicht heute, sagen alle faulen Leute." ("Don't delay what you can do today.") A similar proverb reads "Morgenstunde hat Gold im Munde." ("The morning hour has gold in its mouth.")

   🐜 🐜 🐜

When I was starting my practice in Syracuse, New York, one of my first patients asked me, "What do you think of us Irish electing a Jew Lord Mayor of Dublin?" He meant, of course, Robert Briscoe, who described in his autobiography how he was in his mayoral robes looking out over the St. Patrick's Day Parade and two Jewish women spotted him.

"You see the gentleman in his mayoral robes? He is Robert Briscoe, a Jew who has been elected Lord Mayor of Dublin!" said one of the women.

"Isn't that wonderful," the other woman exclaimed. "And this could only happen in America!"

   🐜 🐜 🐜

A few years ago, when Herta's sister, Lucy, visited with her daughter, Mary Ann, we drove around the Syracuse University section of town. During our ride, Mary Ann asked me if I talked with every woman patient about sex. "I think that is terrible," she said.

I explained that I would definitely discuss the subject if the patient wanted me to. But I was instantly reminded of a psychiatrist many years ago who was attending one of the New York Medical Society meetings. One of the general practitioners tried to be up to date and questioned all his female patients about their sex lives. He asked one of them: "Well, Mrs. Rothenberg [not her real name], what do you think of sex?"

"I tell you Doc, it's one of the finest stores on Fifth Avenue," she answered (meaning, of course, the Saks Fifth Avenue department store).

&   &   &

Here's a talmudic proverb that not too many big business people subscribe to: "Who is rich? He who is satisfied with what he has."

&   &   &

You might have heard about the soldier who needed some hand surgery and was assured by his surgeon that the result would be quite favorable.

"Will I be able to do everything with this hand?" the soldier queried.

"I don't see why not," the doctor replied.

"Will I be able to play the piano?"

"There is no reason why you shouldn't," the doctor answered.

"That's funny," the soldier replied. "I was never able to play the piano before!"

&   &   &

Do you remember those two friends who met one another on the street after a long time apart and one said to the other, "You look very nice. You wear a beautiful suit, but have you noticed that one of your shoes is black and the other is brown?"

"You might laugh," the other man retorted, "But I have another pair at home just like this."

        ♣   ♣   ♣

When, many years ago, I visited Dr. Ernest Schweiger, a cousin of mine who practiced medicine in Portsmouth, Virginia, he told me a story that I shall relate here. He came originally from Vienna, Austria, where his father was a rabbi. One day one of his patients saw in one of the consultation rooms the picture of Dr. Schweiger's grandfather. The patient, a Protestant minister, said to the physician, "Do you see how wrinkled his forehead is and how depressed he looks?" The minister explained to my cousin that the grandfather's unhappy appearance was due to the fact that he "rejected Jesus as his Messiah." Dr. Schweiger replied that his nonbelief was not the reason for his sadness. The real reason was that Protestants persecuted him and his ancestors day and night, and he had no place to rest.

The reverend thought and thought, and finally blurted out, "You know, you have got something there." (This is a true story, and Dr. Forrest commented "great story" on Sarah's paper.)

        ♣   ♣   ♣

The following is a story that made the rounds in Germany when the Nazis were in power. It is the story about two bicyclists, one of them a bigot and an anti-Semite while the other is fairminded. One day the bigot said to his fairminded friend, "You know, the Jews are our misfortune. They are to blame for everything."

"Yes," the fairminded friend replied, "the Jews and the bicyclists."

"Why the bicyclists?" the anti-Semite inquired.

"Why the Jews?" was the response of the fairminded friend.

7

The Jews and the Bible

Most of the anecdotes I recounted had to do with Jews and anti-Semitism. It would be a good thing, then, to write at this point about the Jews and the Bible.

Since my early childhood I had to come to grips with this topic. What better way to start this discussion than with my own *Once a Doctor*. As I write this I have my book in front of me; last night I signed copies at a large bookstore in town with the help of its efficient promotions coordinator, Kim Musselman, whose father is a well-known pediatrician in Ogdensburg, New York.

Any Jewish person who has experienced the Nazi Holocaust has to come to grips with his or her identity. It was the Hebrew Bible that separated the Jews from the Gentile world of Catholics, Protestants, and secularists. As the Jewish philosopher Emil Fackenheim, professor emeritus of philosophy at the University of Toronto, wrote in his *God's Presence in History*: "Jews are forbidden to hand Hitler posthumous victories. They are commanded to survive as Jews, lest the Jewish people perish."

I described in my autobiography the discrimination

against all Jews, and the few of us who were Jewish medical students. I also wrote of "Kristal Nacht" or Crystal Night, when the Nazi's destroyed Jewish-owned businesses and shops. I wrote of my incarceration in the concentration camps, where I was imprisoned together with Catholic priests and Protestant ministers, all of whom happened to have a Jewish grandparent. We had to stay at the camp in Buchenwald at that time, later to be transported to extermination camps such as Auschwitz and Treblinka in Eastern Europe. In *Once a Doctor* I commented on what the camps portended for the Jews in the early years of the Nazi regime:

> This "mild" concentration camp incarceration [at Buchen-wald] had shown us how urgent it was for the Jews to leave Germany as quickly as possible. It was clear that the Nazis intended to get rid of us, which was only right from their diabolic point of view. After all, the Jews had given the Bible to the world, and even the most estranged one remembers the old sayings: "Love your neighbor as yourself"; "You shall not insult the deaf or put a stumbling block before the blind"; "Do not judge your fellow man until you have stood in his place"; and "A person who publicly shames his neighbor is like someone who has shed blood."

All of these Jewish rules did not fit into the Nazi dictionary. So we had to go to the Gestapo once a month to report our "progress."

Earlier I mentioned Robert Coles's wonderful book *The Spiritual Life of Children* in which he discusses the similarities in the ideas about God, destiny, and the afterlife voiced by children with Christian, Jewish, Muslim, or agnostic backgrounds. I have also discovered another little book, this one written by Rabbi Marc Gellman and his friend Monsignor Thomas Hartman, a Catholic priest, published under the title *Where Does God Live?* In simple terms they explain to children how God is found in nature by watching the trees and flowers grow, seeing animals born and develop, and witnessing the purposeful existence of our bodily structures. Virginia Apgar, a well-known researcher, developed the Apgar Score to determine the chances that a newborn baby has to grow into a normal human being. The more Ms. Apgar observed the results of her studies, the more she became convinced that a creative force was at work. As the psalmist says, "A fool says in his heart that there is no God."

According to Gellman and Hartman, another reason for little children to know about God is their "inside voice," which we grown-ups call the conscience. It helps us to distinguish right from wrong. According to the Talmud, every human being has this inner voice; but, if you decide to disregard it there will be a time when you won't hear it anymore.

The third way to find contact with God is through the Bible. The Gellman and Hartman book has been on the best-seller list for many years. It speaks to you if you listen. It will speak to you whether you believe, as some do, that every word of the Bible has been dictated by God to Moses and the later prophets, or, as others do, that those who inscribed the Bible were at best divinely inspired.

In a wonderful 1991 interview by *Time* magazine we learn a lot about the qualifications of psychiatrist Robert Coles. His mother used to take the children to the Episcopal Church. His father was a scientist, a man who was "Jewish with some Catholic background." The father would sit outside and read the Sunday paper. He believed that all the churches "basically betrayed their ideals," and Robert Coles is in agreement with his father.

"Do you believe in a supernatural God?" the reporter asked him.

"Sometimes I do, and at other times I have moments of doubt. I regard those moments of doubt as part of the struggle that we all have for faith."

Now, about two thousand years ago, when Christianity started, the Jews remained Jews, unable to accept all the beliefs and teachings of the New Testament. They remained steadfast to their Hebrew Scriptures. As I have already mentioned, according to the Jewish tradition, the righteous of all nations have a share in the world to come.

About fifteen years ago, at an Interreligious Area Council convention in Syracuse, one of the main speakers was Protestant theologian and Harvard professor Dr. Krister Stendahl. He marveled at Moses Maimonides, the great Jewish philosopher of the Middle Ages, who, in spite of all the Christian and Islamic persecution, was convinced that God created those two religions to help Judaism to mend the world.

Apparently, everything would be fine and well if the fundamentalists of our neighboring religions wouldn't find fault with the Jews and try to convert them. They claim that Christianity is a religion of love, while Judaism is a religion of law. They have been taught in Sunday school that there is no love for animals in the Old Testament and that the Jewish Bible decreed the death penalty far too often. Little do they know that the Torah is called the written law, while later on the Mischnah and the Talmud—what are called the oral law—were created to make Judaism more understandable to the modern reader. I remember that in one of the talmudic discussions the rabbis declared, "A court that decrees the death penalty once in seventy years is called a cruel one."

When in December of 1991 I reviewed *To Be a Jew* by Orthodox Rabbi Hayim Donin, my non-Jewish friends were surprised about the commandments or *mitzvot*: "It is a mitvah [an obligation] to provide for return of a lost object to its rightful owner"; "one must feed and clothe the poor of the gentiles together with the poor of Israel"; and "One who is responsible for feeding animals is forbidden to sit down to eat until he has fed the animals."

🐾 🐾 🐾

Readers might recall that some years ago the leader of the influential Southern Baptist Convention, the Reverend Baily Smith, said in a speech, "Friends, God does not listen to the prayers of a Jew." The speech went virtually unnoticed, that is, until some organizations got a hold of it and made it public. The Jewish community was in an uproar, except for the agnostic Society for Humanistic Judaism, which maintains that God does not listen to anybody's prayer. Subsequently, the reverend went to Israel to apologize for his inconsiderate words. When he returned to his own Baptist church, though, he informed the large congregation that, of course, he meant every word of what he had said with regard to the Jews' prayers.

There has always been a lot of animosity toward the Jews by part of the population because of their status as "Chosen People." The Ku Klux Klan always felt that because of this status, Jews were encouraged to own the presses, the banks, and, finally, to rule the world. A much different view comes from the evangelical/fundamentalist Christians. They had learned in Sunday school that the Jews were originally chosen and given the Covenant by God, but that this Covenant had been taken away from the Jews and transferred to the Christian Church after the "Jewish people had rejected Christ." Although Pope John Paul II has stressed again and again that the Jews of today are not to blame for the death of Jesus, millions were persecuted and died during the Middle Ages, the Spanish Inquisition, and the Holocaust.

The Jewish tradition gives us a much different reason for Israel's "chosenness." It tells us that Israel accepted the Covenant reluctantly, after it had been offered first to all the other nations. When it was offered to the sons of Esau, they asked, "What is written in it?" They were answered with, "Thou shall not commit murder."

"We cannot accept that," they said, for their grandfather, Esau, was told that he would live by the sword.

The Torah was then offered to the sons of Ammon and Moab, and they wanted to know what was in it. "Thou shalt not commit adultery," they were told. They refused to accept it, saying, "We are the descendants of Lot's daughters and our very existence depends on an act of unchastity."

The Holy Law was next offered to the children of Ishmael.

They, too, wanted to know what was in it. "Thou shalt not steal" was the answer. The Ishmaelites refused to accept it, because they claimed that their ancestors had been told that Ishmael's hand would be against every man. And so it went with every nation. This is the explanation for Israel's chosenness (see *The Lore of the Old Testament* by Joseph Gaer).

Compare this to the fundamentalist Christian claims that the original Covenant or chosenness had been taken away from the Jews and transferred to the Christian Church. As Eugene Fisher, director of the National Conference of Catholic Bishops for Catholic-Jewish Relations, declared many years ago at a large convention sponsored by the Syracuse Area Interreligious Council, "It was the general consensus, for centuries and centuries, that God punished the Jewish people for their rejection of Christ, and when the persecution did not get going fast enough, the population helped along a little."

Some readers will remember from *Once a Doctor* how my wife, Herta, was asked by some of her domestic help, "Don't you feel bad, Mrs. Hartmann, that the Jews killed Jesus?" One of our home aides felt the need to ask our friend Eleene—the dear woman who has been with our son, Michael, day and night for over three decades—"Are you Jewish?" When Eleene said no, that she comes from a more liberal Protestant background, the aide continued, "The Jews killed Jesus." When Eleene said that she didn't agree with the statement, the aide was ready to "prove" it to her from the New Testament. It makes me genuinely sick to report this. But there have been far worse experiences.

After my autobiography was published, I asked many of those with whom I correspond, especially those who were evangelical/fundamentalist Christians, to reply to a question I heard once on the old Phil Donahue talk show: "Can a Jew (or a Jewess) who lives a good life, but does not believe in the divinity of Jesus or in his sacrificial death, go to heaven or be saved?" To my absolute horror, these intelligent and basically good people had to look it up in the New Testament, quoting from the Book of Romans, while others blurted it right out—

the Jew had to go to hell. They were not even ashamed of what they were saying. In fact, it was their belief that they had the backing of their New Testament.

Joseph Telushkin, author of *Jewish Literacy,* reprints in his book titled *Uncommon Sense* a story that writer Leo Tolstoy recounts in *My Religion*: "Not long ago I was reading the Sermon on the Mount with a rabbi. At nearly every verse he showed me very similar passages in the Hebrew Bible and the Talmud. When we reached the words, 'Turn the other cheek,' he did not say that this, too, is in the Talmud, but asked with a smile, 'Do the Christians obey this command?' I had nothing to say in reply, especially as at that particular time, Christians, far from turning the other cheek, were smiting the Jews on both cheeks."

To conclude this chapter on a more optimistic note, I'll quote from a letter sent to me by Elli Matthews, one of Sarah and Maurice's teachers at Jamesville Dewitt High School. She was kind enough to give me permission to cite freely:

Dear Dr. Hartmann,

. . . The Holocaust was a tragic nightmare not only for the Jewish people but for every human being. . . . I am a born-again Christian, [but] I cannot believe non-Christians are condemned to hell.

May God bless you. Your book has blessed me.

Very gratefully,

Elli Matthews

8

What Judaism Means

Now that we have come to know the erroneous perceptions of Judaism harbored by other religious denominations, I shall attempt to discuss what Judaism means to the Jew of today.

It was about fifty years ago that we held a discussion group at Temple Concord on the topic of "Basic Judaism," under the leadership of Rabbi Benjamin Friedman. Our guide was Rabbi Milton Steinberg's book bearing the same title. (This wonderful book, published in 1947, was reissued after Rabbi Steinberg's untimely death in 1975.) The volume was written for traditional and more modern Jews, for Christians, Muslims, Buddhists, agnostics, and atheists. Rabbi Steinberg believed that "The righteous of all nations have a share in the world to come."

I am sure that our course at Temple Concord gave us a lasting knowledge of Judaism's essentials. Yet, *Basic Judaism* appeared long before the truly gruesome facts about the Holocaust were yet known. It took decades before a few of the survivors of the extermination camps found the strength to write their memoirs. This interval made it easier for the revisionists to write their Holocaust denial pamphlets.

I have in front of me Benny Krauts wonderful study titled *From Reform Judaism to Ethical Culture: The Religious Evolution of Felix Adler.* Adler, a former Reformed rabbi, had renounced Judaism and started the New York Society for Ethical Culture. He died in 1933, soon after the Hitler regime gained power. If he had lived through all of the Nazi persecutions in Germany, he would have been honest enough to realize that the messianic age, as visualized by the Hebrew prophets, had not yet arrived.

What, then, does Judaism mean for the Jew of today? In answer to this question, I shall focus on a work titled *The Nine Questions People Ask about Judaism,* written by Dennis Prager and Joseph Telushkin. The book, published in 1981, is authored by two men who had been close friends since high school. The Preface contains one of Holocaust survivor Elie Weisel's poignant observations: "The Jew may love God, or he might fight with God, but he may not ignore God." In contrast to other religions, it is not the creed but the deed that counts in Judaism. Prager and Telushkin first ask whether one can doubt God's existence and still be a good Jew. They answer with a definite yes. A great many people believe in some higher power, but the doubter is rather concerned to know if such a power plays any part in our lives, our destiny, or in the prevention of evil. To prove their point that a doubter can still be a good Jew, Prager and Telushkin quote from the Talmud: "Better that they (the Jews) abandon me, but follow my law," for by practicing Judaism's laws, the Jew will return to God.

They also cite a little story about the Hassidic rabbi who was asked why the Lord permits people to deny Him (or Her). "Heresy is purposeful also," the rabbi answered, "for when you confront another who is in need, you should imagine that there is no God to help, but that you alone can meet the man's needs."

How different the opinions are about God and Judaism! I mentioned earlier the philosopher Emil Fackenheim from Toronto who has been living in Jerusalem since his retirement. As a German-born rabbi, he suffered in a German concentration camp. He is the author of many books and has expounded his credo in *The Conditions of Jewish Belief*, originally published by *Commentary* magazine. In *God's Presence in History* Fackenheim offers a chapter titled "The Commanding Voice of Auschwitz" in which he asks "What does the voice of Auschwitz command?" to which he answers: "Jews are forbidden to hand Hitler posthumous victories. They are commanded to survive as Jews, lest the Jewish people perish." From time to time, according to his *Jewish Bible after the Holocaust*, Professor Fackenheim returns to Germany to participate in Jewish-Christian dialogue. Many of the young women and men who attend these dialogues grapple with serious questions: Why had Christianity failed during the Holocaust? Why had it not come to the Jews' defense?

₳ ₳ ₳

I believe it was in Atlantic City, while I was attending an annual meeting of the American Medical Association (I only went to these meetings if they were held in the eastern art of the country, near my home), that I happened to read Richard Rubenstein's *After Auschwitz*. The chapter that impressed me most was the one titled "The Dean and the Chosen People." Rabbi Rubenstein, who has also contributed to *Commentary*'s collected work *Conditions of Jewish Belief*, interviewed Heinrich Greuber, Dean of the Evangelical Church of East and West Berlin. The interview took place at Greuber's home in Berlin-Dahlem. This remarkable man had placed not only his own life but that of his family in danger many times to help the Jews in Nazi Germany. Yet this man's quotes from the Hebrew Scriptures and the New Testament changed Rabbi Rubenstein's idea of God completely.

Dr. Greuber insisted that somehow the Nazi slaughter of the Jews was "God's will," that God was instrumental in the Holocaust, that "because the Jews are God's Chosen People, God wanted Hitler to punish them." This man, who was rightly honored by many Jewish and world organizations for his resistance to the Nazis, had no trouble finding passages from his New Testament and from some prophets to justify his view that "God wanted the Nazis to destroy the Jews."

For Richard Rubenstein all this was hard to take, and he felt that the Jewish community should not hold on to the doctrine of the election of Israel. I am no theologian, but I don't think anything can help people who take the Bible literally. And surprisingly, there is a small ultra-Orthodox Jewish splinter group—the only Jewish group of its kind—whose members believe that the Holocaust was designed to punish the Jews for not following all the commandments of the Torah. Needless to say, the great majority of the Jewish people consider such an idea "obscene."

This reminds me of an article I read years ago in the well-written secular humanist magazine *Free Inquiry*. The author, a young Orthodox rabbi, claimed that the Holocaust was God's punishment for the sins of the Jewish people. A fierce rebuttal by noted agnostic philosopher Sidney Hook soon appeared in a future issue of the magazine. It was also at this time that I read an interesting interview with Sidney Hook conducted by *Commentary*'s editor Norman Podhoretz titled "On Being a Jew." The interview was conducted in October 1990, about nine months before Hook's death.

Unfortunately, Hook had no real Jewish education, and although he didn't like some of the things in the Bible, he was proud of his heritage. He was also interested in resisting anti-Semitism, fighting against the infamous Father Coughlin and against the likes of Mortimer Adler, who was trying to convert Jewish boys to Catholicism. Hook felt uncomfortable reading "about someone like [Louis] Farakhan, and the huge audiences he attracts." Sidney Hook's grandchildren had no Jewish education, a fact the philosopher regretted very much, because they also had no Jewish consciousness.

Hook's case reminds me of the well-known critic and English lecturer David Daiches, who taught at Cambridge University and, for a number of years, in the United States at the University of Chicago and at Cornell. Daiches spent his boyhood years in Scotland, where his father, an Orthodox rabbi, was the head of the Edinburgh Jewish community. Gradually, David did not find much sense in Jewish ritual; he did not agree with some of the biblical stories and eventually he became an agnostic. His father's attempts to answer David's concerns about Judaism never quite satisfied his son, but the young man always loved his father very much. When studying at the University of Edinburgh, David fell in love with a non-Jewish coed, whom he later married. He remained an agnostic and did not bring up his children in any particular religious tradition.

I read about the professor and his spiritual problems first in *Commentary* magazine, where an essay titled "My Father and His Father" appeared in December 1955 as a condensation of Daiches's autobiographical work titled *Two Worlds: A Jewish Childhood in Edinburgh.* In this book the author is full of warmth and love for his father. "My father was greater than his works. Indeed, his life was his work, and to separate the two is to do both an injustice. Once, asked whether he believed in personal immortality, he smiled and said that one lived most effectively after death in the memories of those whom one has loved and taught."

This certainly doesn't seem very Orthodox to me, and I agree with the beautiful *New York Times* review by the well-known late writer Maurice Samuel, who asks whether it was not possible for David to rephrase his father's faith "in terms which are more acceptable to a warm Judaism and to a modern intellectual." But David Daiches seems to belong to the ". . . all or nothing school. He will not tamper with his father's orthodoxy. He would rather reject it than reinterpret it." And Samuel closes his review with this question: "Mr. Daiches's parents, grounded in the Jewish religion, seem to have brought up very decent children. Will Mr. Daiches's children, brought up, it seems, in no particular religion, be able to do the same?"

Yes, David Daiches lived between two worlds. And so did Oswald Rufeisen, whose story is told in a wonderful book by Nechama Tec, herself a Holocaust survivor and a professor of sociology at the University of Connecticut at Stamford.

Rufeisen told the Nazis in occupied Poland that he was half German and half Polish. He was somehow able to get work as a translator for the German police. Whenever he heard about some intended action against the Jews, he would notify the intended victims, thereby saving the lives of hundreds of Jews. When his Jewish identity was finally discovered, he found refuge in a convent next door to the police station where he was working. In the convent Rufeisen changed his faith and converted to Catholicism. Apparently, he had been reading about some miraculous cures attributed to the interventions of the Virgin Mary. He defined himself as a Christian Jew and later became a Carmelite monk and moved to Israel. Nechame Tec wrote the only authorized biography of Father Daniel, as he is now called.

After his emigration to Israel, Father Daniel went to court claiming that he was a Jew, even though he had become a Catholic. He wanted to be allowed to put the word "Jew" in his passport. Four of the five High Court justices denied his request. Everybody loved him in Israel, and everybody loves him now and admires what he did for the Jewish people in Nazi-occupied Poland. This is what presiding Judge Moshe Silberg essentially said in his decision:

> We see before us a man who, in the darkest days of the Holocaust . . . endangered his life many times for his Jewish brothers. How can we deny such a person his deepest quest . . . to completely fuse with the people that he loves? . . . Father Daniel is really asking us to nullify the historical sanctified meaning of the word Jew and to completely turn our backs on the spiritual values for which we have been giving our lives daily.

Though he was denied the right to call himself a Jew, Father Daniel was granted Israeli citizenship.

Oswald Rufesien (aka Father Daniel) emphasizes that he is a Hebrew Christian, and they don't proselytize. When asked if there is any connection between Hebrew Christians and the

Jews for Jesus, he says that the latter are Jews in the United States "with present-day ideas about Jesus," as represented by Protestant sects, while he is a "universal Christian."

When, under Mikhail Gorbachev, Jews were finally permitted to leave Russia and the old Soviet Union to start a new life in Israel or the United States, they wanted to learn more about Judaism. Among others, the Jews for Jesus went over to Russia to "teach" them, and the Russia Jews, unfamiliar with Judaic tradition and scripture, thought they were learning the real Judaism, that is, until they found out the truth. You see, the split occurred two thousand years ago, and you have to either be a Jew or a Christian; there is nothing in-between. It was Dennis Prager who told us in his *Ultimate Issues* that in talking about the Jews for Jesus movement one might just as well talk about "Christians for Mohammed" or "Vegetarians for Meat."

Father Daniel works in Israel now as a tourist guide, and he is often invited to schools to talk to Jewish children about Christianity. He loves Israel and appreciates the tolerance of its people. Some of Father Daniel's friends are convinced that he will return to Judaism. When Nechama Tec repeated those rumors to him, he smiled and said, "But how can I return? I never left!"

In 1988 a book was written by Howard Simons titled *Jewish Times: Voices of the American-Jewish Experience.* Of its most interesting interviews is one with William S. Cohen, then Republican U.S. Senator from Maine. Son of an Irish mother and a Jewish father, he went to Hebrew School from the time he was six. When he was thirteen years old he was told that he could not be bar mitzvahed unless his mother converted to Judaism or until he went through a special conversion ceremony himself. Cohen was very angry. They should have told him in the beginning, not after seven years of Hebrew School.

Later, he played basketball very well when he was attending Bangor High School. In fact, he scored thirty-three points on one occasion. The headline read "Coyne Scores 33."

The Jewish community was in a bit of an uproar. They felt his name had been deliberately misspelled.

William Cohen, now our distinguished secretary of defense, loves both his Irish mother and his Jewish father, who is a baker and "a wonderful human being." He said his father would only go to shul on the high holidays, but he was "very committed to the principles of being Jewish." Cohen became an attorney and in 1972 and later he decided to run for Congress. He was advised that he could never be elected with a name like Cohen. But he was (in fact, he later became a U.S. Senator), and today he claims that "bigotry is not a factor at all." Yet he does not seem convinced that everything is all right now. For example, he does not want his children to have the same experiences he had. "I have a [son] Kevin and a [son] Christopher, and [their first names are] sort of to offset the name [Cohen] as such, because immediately everyone knows they're not Jewish. So, they don't have to deal with that." What a shame that such deception is thought to be necessary in the United States in this modern age.

In this connection I would like to return for a moment to Rabbi Richard Rubenstein, whose *After Auschwitz* I have already discussed. He had only a minimal Hebrew education, and his parents opposed his having a bar mitzvah. During his childhood he was called a dirty Jew and beaten up by some drunken gang after a high school dance. He wanted to rid himself of "a seemingly meaningless Jewish burden," so he studied theology to become a Unitarian clergyman. He met some very helpful Unitarian ministers, one of whom explained that while Unitarianism is close to Reform Judaism, there remained "some residual anti-Semitism in the Unitarian Churches." This friend also insisted that Rubenstein would have a better chance of success as a Unitarian minister if he changed his name from Rubenstein to a "less obviously Jewish name." This he refused to do. Rubenstein was admitted to Hebrew Union College to become a Reformed rabbi, but turned eventually to a more traditional Judaism.

ꙮ   ꙮ   ꙮ

According to Jonathan Kaufman's book *Broken Alliance* and the daily press reports, Jews were always in the forefront of the Civil Rights Movement. The famous Jewish theologian Abraham Joshua Heschel marched in the South in the 1960s along with other leaders of the Jewish faith, arm in arm with Reverend Martin Luther King Jr., to protest the oppression of blacks. Unfortunately, in recent years, scurrilous charges have been raised by demagogues against the Jewish community. The Jewish people never had any feeling of superiority vis a vis blacks. They had been taught for thousands of years from Hebrew Scriptures with the words of the prophet Micah: "He has told you, O man, what is good, and what the Lord requires of you. Only to do justice and to love goodness, and walk humbly with your God."

In this connection it is interesting to speak of the Falashahs, a group of black Jews living for centuries in Ethiopia. They had a desire several years ago to emigrate to Israel so they and their children could learn more about Judaism. In an unprecedented airlift during one of the Ethiopian famines, thousands and thousands of black Jews were flown to Israel within twenty-four hours. They now work in the same jobs as the rest of the population, and their children attend the same schools as all the other children. This is to be expected.

ꙮ   ꙮ   ꙮ

I mentioned before how Rabbi Charles Sherman of Temple Adath Yeshurun had discussed my autobiography during one of his Friday night services, which he called "Services under the Stars." But here I refer to another review, given by Rabbi Sherman about a year later. On this occasion I was accompanied by my friend Bill Lynch, a Jesuit seminarian, who eventually left the Jesuit order but continues to teach in Catholic high schools.

(He shared with me the reason for his break with the Jesuit order. When his mother, whom he loved dearly, contracted a terminal illness, Bill wanted to spend as much time with her as possible. But he did not receive much understanding from his Jesuit superiors. Just at the time of her most critical stage, the Jesuit hierarchy wanted to send Bill away to another college. If he had followed these orders, he would not have been able to care for his mother during her final days.)

Bill was happy when I met him in Syracuse for the service. I can recall when he came to our house and met our son, Michael, for the first time. He looked at our physically disabled and mentally retarded boy and remarked that Michael brings out the ability to love in people. We could not have agreed with him more.

The book that Rabbi Sherman chose to review during his service at Temple Adath was Julius Lester's *Lovesong: Becoming a Jew.* Julius Lester, a black man and the son of a Southern Methodist minister, disagreed with the religiosity of his father at an early age. Julius had strong atheistic leanings. After moving to New York City, he supported himself by folksinging and teaching the guitar and banjo. In early 1968 his first book appeared, as I am reminded again by the beautiful *New York Times* review by Joel Oppenheimer. Lester called it *Look Out Whitey! Black Power's Gon' Get Your Mama!* Julius Lester would later moderate a weekly radio show, but he became really famous when he interviewed a militant black history teacher who recited (at his request) a poem by a fourteen-year-old girl from one of his classes. Lester urged the teacher, named Les Campbell, that it was important for people to know the "feelings being aroused in at least one black child" because of some school conflict in Ocean Hill, Brownsville. The poem began:

> Hey, Jewboy, with that yarmulke on your head
> You-pale-faced Jewboy-I wish your were dead.

Actually, the poem was much, much longer, but didn't contribute any more to brotherhood than the first two lines. At the same time, Mr. Lester was on a spiritual journey and was attracted to the philosopher Friedrich Nietzsche. Later on he leaned toward Thomas Merton later on. While on his search, he remembered that "his great-grandfather on his mother's side was a German Jew named Altschul." Gradually, Julius Lester found his own identity in Judaism (as described in his *Lovesong*), and he regretted the fact that all the other descendants of Adolph Altschul had converted to Christianity. He acknowledged himself as "the only Jew in the family." Now he belongs to a conservative Jewish congregation and teaches African-American and Judaic Studies at the University of Massachusetts in Amherst. I only know Julius Lester from his book, but I have personal knowledge of another black man, right here in Syracuse. His name is Nat Footman.

Nat Footman was the custodian of the Temple Society of Concord, his only job since he moved North many years ago. He helped the congregants whenever there were minor problems. He aided disabled people who might be stuck in the small elevator, or he would seat and serve them at dinner parties. He also took care to see that the children had a good breakfast before Hebrew or Sunday school began. When necessary he would employ his gentle persuasion to steer them toward their classes.

Nat Footman served Temple Concord for twenty-five years, and he would have stayed on longer had it not been for his heart condition, from which he never recovered. But none of us will ever forget the memorable Friday night service on June 19, 1992, in honor of his retirement. The temple was filled to capacity. I estimate that half of the guests were members of Temple Concord Congregation, while the rest were family members and congregants of his own large Protestant church.

We shared our prayer books together; we sang in Hebrew (with English transliteration), or in English. As Rabbi Ezring remarked on more than one occasion, visitors from any faith can agree with at least 90 percent of the Jewish prayer book.

In a later "thank you" note, Mr. Footman expressed his admiration to our cantor Fancine Berg and to the choir "for the beautiful rendition of 'Amazing Grace.'" It was easy to tell to which congregation the many worshippers on that night belonged. Even if you were color blind you would notice that the men belonging to the Reformed Temple Concord wore no skullcaps, while all the black men did. I am sure that they had been guests of conservative or orthodox congregations before.

Aside from Rabbi Ezring and the minister of his church, there were several other speakers honoring Mr. Footman. And the guest of honor gave a humorous reply. One speaker, attorney R. Engel, a former president of Temple Society of Concord, told the story of the children in the Sunday school who adored the honored custodian. One day their teacher asked the pupils to draw a picture of one of the heroes of Jewish history. One child drew a picture of Abraham, another chose to draw Moses, while a third one drew the likeness of King David. Others seemed more interested in the likes of Job, Queen Esther, or Ruth. But one of the pupils designed a life-sized portrait of Nat Footman. I think Mr. Footman considered this portrait one of the highest honors he ever received!

9

Retracing History

Not long ago I received a letter from the International Tracing and Information Service of the American Red Cross in which they indicated—for the first time in fifty years—that they did indeed possess some small details not only about the fate of my father and mother at the hands of the Nazis but about the fate of Herta's mother as well. All were Jews deported by Hitler's government. No information had been available about my sister, Kaete, or Herta's younger brother and his small family. The Red Cross letter offered these morsels of information:

> Johanna Friedmann née Neufeld was delivered from Breslau to the Ghetto Theresienstadt on 27 July 1942; transferred to Concentration Camp Auschwitz on 15 May 1944.
>
> Sarah Hartmann née Blick and Moritz Hartmann were delivered from Breslau to the Ghetto Theresienstadt on 27 July 1942.
>
> We are still awaiting a response regarding Erwin Friedmann.
>
> We regret to inform you that no information is available about Kaete Weiss Fisch née Hartmann.

This new Holocaust and War Victims Tracing and Information Center in Baltimore, Maryland, opened after the former Soviet Union released documents containing the names of four hundred thousand Holocaust victims. I applied for information in the fall of 1990, and in March of 1992 a very descriptive interview by contributing writer Kelly Clark appeared in the *Syracuse Post Standard.* A picture of me (as on so many occasions) was taken by photographer David Lassman in my library, with a copy of *Once a Doctor* in the foreground.

This late release of the documents by the former Soviet Union is another reason so many of the survivors had not heard anything about the fate of their close relatives. This gave the Holocaust deniers and revisionists a reason to talk of the "hoax of the twentieth century." Unfortunately, there have been many people in the United States and Canada who agree with these revisionists. You will recall my discussion of how Christian fundamentalists believe that the Jews deserved their fate because they were being punished for not recognizing Jesus as the son of God—the Messiah who died for their sins. Once in a while, one of my Christian fundamentalist correspondents admonishes me: "Your have to forgive and forget." With these words they forgive the Nazis for what they did to the Jews. Needless to say, I harbor no ill-feelings toward the new German generation, and many of the potential German publishers who have read my autobiography know this.

After the Red Cross information came in, I sent copies to my few surviving relatives. The information is far from complete, though the agency said it would notify me as soon as new data became available. The question for those who read Holocaust reports and books is always the same: "Why remain Jewish and endanger the children and further generations if, God forbid, another Holocaust should ever happen?" If the children wish to change, and Judaism not longer means anything to them, they have a perfect right to convert to any other religion or choose not to believe altogether. They may intermarry and give up their Jewish identity. I made it clear elsewhere that I never intend to give up my Jewish identity.

        🐚   🐚   🐚

One of the first books by a Holocaust survivor was one written by our good friend Judith Sternberg Newman. *In the Hell of Auschwitz* came out in 1963, and is now in its third printing. Like Herta, Judith was a nurse at the Breslau Jewish Hospital, but in February 1942 she was taken with ten thousand other Jews to the concentration camp at Auschwitz. Of all those people, she was one of just thirty-eight who survived to tell her story. Judith's mother, sisters, brother, and fiancé perished in the death camp.

As a reviewer for the *Syracuse Jewish Observer,* I became familiar with such books as *The Rescue of the Danish Jews,* edited by Leo Goldberger, and Susan Zuccotti's two books, *The Italians and the Holocaust* and *The Holocaust and the French.* Protestant Denmark and Catholic Italy were two European countries where the highest percentage of Jewish lives were saved. The Jews of Denmark were brought to safety by their Christian friends, then taken in boats during the night to neutral Sweden, where they survived the war. In Italy it was easy for Jews to mix with the general population, since they blended into the indigenous population. But the Italians also refused to listen to authority; they balked when they were told to round up Jews.

Even in France, under the Vichy government, more Jewish lives were saved than in the other European countries, mainly due to benign neglect. The French just never reported Jews who lived in their midst. And who could forget the story of the village of LeChambon and its pastor who, with his family, risked their lives harboring many Jews who sought refuge from the Gestapo. This mountain village of three thousand organized to save about five thousand Jewish children and adults from certain annihilation. A few years ago, Philip Hallie, a professor of ethics, spoke at one of the local Syracuse synagogues on Holocaust Memorial Day. Professor Hallie was so moved by the story of the village of LeChambon that he spent several months there in the 1970s. In 1989 the first edition of his *Lest Innocent Blood Be Shed* was published, and I am fortunate to have an autographed copy.

Every year, in the town of Yad Vashem in Israel, many people from Europe are honored as "Righteous Gentiles," who have saved Jewish lives without regard for their own. How strange that now in Poland, where the Jewish population has dwindled from 3.5 million to fewer than 4,400, there is more anti-Semitism than before the liberation. When times are bad, the forces of intolerance always need a "scapegoat." A 1990 *Newsweek* article titled "The Long Shadow" describes anti-Semitism in postwar Europe. Who doesn't remember the anti-Semitic tirades of Cardinal Jozef Glemp? Pope John Paul II, himself born and raised in Poland, declared in a number of speeches that anti-Semitism is a sin. Let us hope that the pope's good will can bring a change in the attitude of those religious people who still harbor prejudices!

Let us not forget that there is anti-Semitism also in our own country. Soon after I had arrived in the United States, I read the *Lyon's Den,* written by newspaper columnist Leonard Lyons, who described one of the lavish New York parties he attended. One of the guests, a native born American, told the others that it really was not so bad for the Jews in Germany under Hitler—and if it was, then it was well-deserved. One of the listeners, a little Jewish emigre who was visibly angered, screamed at him: "Why don't you go back to Nazi Germany, where I come from?"

10

Why Maintain Judaism?

There has to be a special reason for today's Jew to continue Judaism for himself and for future generations. To understand that reason we must go back to Prager and Telushkin's *Nine Questions People Ask about Judaism.* We have already established that a Jew who declares himself (herself) to be an atheist or agnostic is still considered a Jew according to Jewish law. Just recently I was rereading the transcript of a 1989 daytime talk show featuring the group known as Jews for Jesus. The guests were group members Susan Perlman and Tuyva Zaretsky, Rabbi James Rudin, and the Reverend Philip Culbertson, a life-long expert in Jewish Studies. The Jews for Jesus were unable to understand why Jews consider an atheist a Jew, but "Messianic Jews" are not accepted into the Jewish fold. It is really quite simple. If they would call themselves "Christian" as other converted Jews have done, no one would argue with them. But you cannot believe like the Christians do and then call yourself a Jew just because you celebrate a few Jewish holidays and observe a few Jewish ceremonies now and again. You are either a Jew or a Christian. You must make a choice some time.

In a subsequent chapter Prager and Telushkin ask why it is not enough just to be a good person. Why do we need all these Jewish laws? But to be good, it is not enough never to have hurt anyone; one must be willing to take a stand on behalf of others. The authors quote from the Book of Leviticus: "Do not stand idly by while your neighbor's blood is shed," and from Deuteronomy: "Justice, justice you shall pursue." Just not hurting another person is not enough. If it were, we would have to consider most ordinary Germans during the Holocaust to be good people since they never took action to hurt anyone. The Jew is commanded to do good—to give charity, to silence gossip, and to visit the sick. For example, those who try to give laughter and happiness to people in need of a psychological lift deserve our praise and recognition.

The authors of *The Nine Questions* discuss whether secularists can be completely ethical. Of course they can, and quite often they more ethical than some religious folk. The reason is that we often label people religious as long as they attend services regularly and observe all the ceremonies, irrespective of their ethical standards. Many people who are irreligious or secular are quite ethical; in fact, some are "naturally good," according to Prager and Telushkin. But just as music must be systematically taught if one is to be a musician, so, too, goodness must be systematically taught if we are to produce good people. The secularist received his moral values form his ancestors, whose ethics were inherited from "thousands of years of religion."

Later in *The Nine Questions,* the authors explore the differences between Judaism and humanism. The humanist, in contrast to the the religious person who follows the Hebrew Scriptures, believes in reason. But reason, as the authors say, is "amoral." Few people in Nazi dominated Europe found it "reasonable" to oppose Nazi atrocities. Attempts to do so were often fatal. In addition to reason, humanists have great faith in secular education. Sigmund Freud wrote in *The Future of an Illusion* that "civilization has little to fear from educated people." A few years later he found out otherwise. By that time he had seen how the intellectuals allowed the atrocities of the Third Reich to occur.

In 1959 a symposium was held under the sponsorship of *Free Inquiry,* the leading humanist magazine, under the heading "Jesus in History and Myth." There were Christian, Jewish, and agnostic speakers on the platform, all very careful not to violate the legitimate rights of each other or their fundamentalist critics. As Andrei Sakharov—the most famous of the secular humanists of the twentieth century—stressed in an interview with Paul Kurtz after his liberation from prison, he would never attack religion after experiencing the persecution of all religions in the totalitarian Soviet state.

The paper that appealed to me most was the one titled "A Remonstrance in Concluding," given by John Hick, an English theologian. Hick had started out as a fundamentalist Christian, but he grew out of it. He is a liberal Christian now, and this is what he said:

> Having said that Christianity provides a good framework for the religious life, I do not go on to say that it provides a better framework than all the other world religions. Rather, for many of us it is the framework into which we were born, . . . which suits us better than a framework that is alien to us. Accordingly, I do not seek to convert people of the other great world religions to Christianity, though I would be very happy if I could convert secular humanists to any one of the great world religions. . . .

This statement of Reverend Hick did not please some who considered themselves "secular humanists," for if they hear from somebody who is religiously or spiritually inclined, they don't believe that the person can really be a good humanist. Yet, many of the signers of the *Humanist Manifesto,* such as Joseph Blau, Mordecai Kaplan, and Sol Gordon, have been or are committed Jews.

I recall an article in *Free Inquiry*'s spring issue of 1990 titled "Why I am Not a Jew," by David Dworkin, a computer programmer/analyst. He believes that most Jews consider the Holocaust a divine punishment. We have confronted this view before, at which time I stated that the claim is only thought to be true for a small number of ultra-Orthodox Jews. Dworkin also feels that the majority of Jews see automatically an anti-Semite in every gentile. In my letter to the editor, I reminded Mr. Dworkin and his readers that this is not so. They should fight an anti-Semite when necessary, but they should never forget the great number of "righteous gentiles" who saved Jewish lives during the time of persecution.

I appreciated *Free Inquiry*'s willingness to print my letter, especially since the space for reader responses is often limited. There were six replies, all of them critical, except for one woman who asked why there should be any difficulty for Mr. Dworkin, who just wanted to leave the faith of his ancestors. There isn't any difficulty. Nobody is stopping him.

In the fall 1993 issue of *Free Inquiry,* more than three years after Dworkin's essay appeared, Sheldon Gottlieb, professor of biological sciences at the University of South Alabama, wrote a profound article titled "Why I Am a Humanist-Skeptic—and Still a Jew." He received as a child a thoroughly Orthodox Jewish education "based on the centrality of ethics with emphasis on the rational wisdom of Rabbi Hillel." Gottlieb identifies with the wisdom of Rabbi Hillel, who was asked once by a nonbeliever to recite the entire Torah, while standing on one foot. He responded: "That which is hateful to you, do not do to your neighbor. The rest is commentary. Now go study." The professor studied talmudic and post-talmudic literature as he grew older, and he was intrigued to find in the talmudic book *The Sayings of the Fathers* (Pirkei Avot) another well-known quotation by Rabbi Hillel: "If I am not for myself, who is for me? But, being only for myself, what am I then? And, if not now, when?" Gottlieb celebrates many Jewish holidays. "I respect and selectively practice many aspects of Jewish ritual, not because of their deistic mandates, but because of their great humanistic and ethical values." He is a skeptical Jew and a better humanist because of it!

In this connection there comes to mind the Society for Humanistic Judaism, founded by Rabbi Sherwin Wine about three decades ago. His first congregation was the Birmingham Temple in the suburb of Detroit. A secular humanist and self-styled "ignostic" (a term invented by American humanist Paul Kurtz), Wine was denounced by many as "the atheist rabbi." According to Wine, what you believe or don't believe about God's existence makes no difference in your ethical practice. He identifies strongly with the Jewish people, but he and the members of his congregation do not worship God at Schabat Services. A very illuminating interview with Wine was published in a July 1985 issue of the *Jerusalem Post.* It bore the heading "Saturday the Rabbi Had Nothing to Worship." In it Wine said: ". . . at our temple, where we don't find the Torah very useful, our service will include readings and meditations based on other Jewish sources . . . which might center on the writing of Bialik . . . Ahad Ha'am . . . or Sholem Aleichem. . . ." I have read Rabbi Wine's work titled *Humanistic Judaism* and his journal by the same name, as well as his *Judaism Beyond God,* and I still wonder what difference there is between a secular humanist and a humanistic Jew.

It is really so simple. I would recommend that everyone read *Finding God: Ten Jewish Responses* by Rabbi Rifat Sonsino and Daniel B. Syme. Reformed and conservative Jewish leaders have recommended this book as a study guide. And many of the respondents are at least as open and liberal as the most radical, agnostic, and humanistic secularist. I shall not go into details here, but I will offer you the titles of the ten chapters:

1. God in the Bible
2. God in Rabbinic Literature
3. Philo's Spiritual Monotheism
4. The Neo-Aristotelianism of Maimonides
5. The Mysticism of Luria
6. The Pantheism of Spinoza
7. The Philosophy of Dialogue of [Martin] Buber
8. The Limited Theism of [Milton] Steinberg

9. The Religious Naturalism of [Mordecai] Kaplan
10. The Humanism of [Erich] Fromm

I am not a theologian, but since childhood I have received instruction in the Bible and in some rabbinic literature. I read some books about Moses Maimonides, Baruch Spinoza, and Mordecai Kaplan. I studied Milton Steinberg and reviewed the three volumes of Martin Buber's *Life and Work* by Maurice Friedman. Yet somehow I feel close to Erich Fromm, the psychotherapist who was born in 1900 into an Orthodox Jewish family. He studied in Frankfurt, Germany, under Martin Buber and Franz Rosenzweig and fled to the United States in 1933 when Hitler came to power. Fromm considered himself a "Radical Humanist," and I was especially fascinated by his *You Shall Be as Gods: Radical Interpretation of the Old Testament and Its Tradition,* a warm and learned book showing us how in Judaism the idea of God changed from that of a lawgiver to a God with whom man can deal on terms of equality.

In Fromm's book I read a little story which I later discovered had been anthologized in several places. This talmudic story tells us that in a discussion about ritual cleanliness Rabbi Eliezer brought forth every imaginable argument, but the other rabbis did not accept him. Then Rabbi Eliezer said, "If I am right, this carob tree will prove it." Then, the carob tree was torn a hundred cubits out of its place. "No proof can be brought from a carob tree," the other rabbis retorted. Then Eliezer said, "Let the stream prove it." Thereupon the stream flowed backwards. "No proof can be brought from a stream of water," the rabbis replied. There was still another argument, but finally Rabbi Eliezer said to them: "If Halakhah agrees with me, let it be proved from Heaven!" Thereupon a heavenly voice cried out, "Why do you dispute with Rabbi Eliezer, seeing that in all matters the Halakhah agrees with him?" But Rabbi Joshua arose and exclaimed, "It is not in Heaven!" What he meant by that was that the Torah had been given at Mount Sinai, and we don't pay attention to heavenly voices. Man now deals with God "on terms of equality," a far cry from the authoritative God of Adam and Eve, who were expelled from paradise because they dared to question the authoritative word of God.

Some of my secularist friends might tell me that they find Fromm's story unbelievable. "Don't you know that God's death has been proven a long time ago?" Well, I was reading and rereading *The Death of God* by Gabriel Vahanian, formerly a professor at Syracuse University. According to his presentation, the death of God means that man lives in this "post-Christian era," as if God does not exist.

What has Erich Fromm to say about this question of God's death? In *You Shall Be as God* he writes: "Instead of asking whether God is dead, we might better raise the question whether man is dead. . . . He is in danger of becoming a thing, of being more and more alienated, of losing sight of the real problems of human existence, and of no longer being interested in the answers to these problems."

🐜   🐜   🐜

A few years ago, Judy Petsonk and Jim Remsen, authors of *The Intermarriage Handbook,* spent a weekend as scholars in residence at Temple Society of Concord in Syracuse. Jim Rensen, a former Methodist, is married to a Jewish woman and helps with the Jewish upbringing of their three children. Mrs. Petronk is a Jewish-Conservative who is not intermarried, but she has given advice to several intermarried family members. Their book refers to and recommends Paul Kurtz's *In Defense of Secular Humanism.* "If you are a secularist," they say, "and your partner is a believer or a seeker, don't look down your nose at her [him]. . . . Try to look at yourself over time. Rationalism may be your lifelong credo. But it may also be a stage you are passing through. At some other time, you may develop a need to seek a spiritual dimension in your life."

At the end of their weekend, Petronk and Remsen guided a lively study group at Temple Concord. A nice young intermarried couple with a little baby wanted to ask some questions. The

wife came from a Catholic background, the husband was of
Jewish origin, and they had to decide if the mother should convert to Judaism or how to bring up the child in the Jewish faith.
A short time before the study group met, a nun had pleaded with
the young wife to have her baby baptized as soon as possible so
that the child wouldn't "go to hell." The young mother became
so disgusted that she broke from the Catholic Church at that
moment. (We realize that none of our modern-day Catholics
have this perception of hell or punishment of innocent young
babies anymore.) Still, the wife continued to have her spiritual
yearnings. Whenever she brought to her husband's attention her
religious doubts and uncertainties he managed to steer the topic
of conversation to the latest football game.

Again, it is so important that the secular partner in any
marriage does not look down on the "religious" partner who is
unable to live by reason alone. After all, there are millions and
millions of believers who try to lead a spiritual life, searching
for meaning with the help of Scriptures. And they are not igno-
rant, irrational, or wrongheaded.

&   &   &

Can the members of the Christian religious right or the leaders
of the old Moral Majority understand the Jewish people and be
friends to them? Unfortunately, they can not. Years ago, when
Menachim Begin was prime minister of Israel, some writers
encouraged their fellow Jews to work hand in hand with the
Reverend Jerry Falwell (then leader of the Moral Majority)
because he was so pro-Israel. Later, when an Israeli award was
given to Falwell, Senator Frank Church refused to accept the
same honor on that occasion. More and more people now
realize that the traditional perception of Israel by the Jewish
people differs completely from the one held by the evangelical
fundamentalists. The latter's support of Israel is based upon
their religious beliefs. They don't believe in a secure and independent Jewish state that can live in peace with its neighbors.
They insist that there can be no peace in the Middle East until

"Christ returns." And only after a long struggle ending in the destruction of many Jews or their final conversion will the messianic age be upon us. From time to time some Christian fundamentalist sects announce the end of the world as a time to be followed by the messianic age. But since the Jews want to continue as Jews, the fundamentalists blame them for not converting and for interfering with the Christian version of the "Second Coming" of Christ.

🐜 🐜 🐜

About two years ago, I attended a meeting in Syracuse sponsored by the Jews for Judaism. The speaker was Rabbi Tovia Singer from Teaneck, New Jersey, whose goal it was to help converted Jews return to Judaism. He is frequently begged by teary-eyed mothers to regain their college-educated sons and daughters who were told by missionaries that soon they would become "more complete" Jews. The girls (or boys) were always ready to sit down and listen to Rabbi Singer. One of them—let us call her "Annette"—gave him the reason for breaking with her Jewish faith. She read in the New Testament a prayer that had overwhelmed her. It was a prayer she had never found in any other source: "You shall love the Lord your God with all your mind, with all your strength, with all your being. Set these words, which I command you this day, upon your heart. Teach them faithfully to your children; speak them in your home and on your way, when you lie down and when you rise up. . . ." Rabbi Singer then showed her the original commandment in the Jewish prayer book and in the Hebrew Torah, from which it is originally taken, and "Annette" returned to Judaism, which she has never left since.

When I attended the Syracuse University talk by Rabbi Singer, I met Ms. Cherie Lewis, who had talked in the discussion after the lecture. She was a professor at Los Angeles College and a visiting professor at Syracuse University's Newhouse School of Communications. (My family and I met with her many times, until she went on a study grant to Egypt and

Israel before returning to her teaching duties in California.) One book Cherie Lewis highly recommended was *When God Becomes a Drug: Breaking the Chains of Religious Addiction and Abuse.* The book was written by Father Leo Booth, vicar of St. George Episcopal Church in Hawthorne, California. Father Leo, a recovering alcoholic, suffered also from a compulsive religious addiction. He finds this combination of the two addictions in most of the people he treats. The author's position corresponds with the opinion voiced by Erich Fromm in *You Shall Be as Gods*: "Religions and belief systems seem to be divided into two camps: Those that believe that human nature is essentially good and focus on our innate dignity, and those that maintain that humans are inherently evil and base."

            🐜   🐜   🐜

One of the evangelical preachers I have always admired is Reverend Billy Graham. He certainly is a far cry from those Christian fundamentalists who condemn anyone who doesn't believe exactly as they do. Needless to say, the Jewish people cannot agree with his religious convictions, but for decades he has been invited by the various presidents of Israel to preach his message there, as long as he didn't try to convert Jews. Once, as I recall, when asked what he would be if he were not born a Christian, Graham replied that he could very well live as a Jew. Naturally, the Hebrew Bible is his Bible, too.

In an essay in the November 15, 1993 issue of *Time* magazine, on the occasion of Graham's seventy-fifth birthday, he was quoted extensively on many subjects. He said that "God does not dwell in a body, so we cannot define Him in a material way. God is a spirit. I have had tremendous messages from Him, which are from the Bible." On Scripture he notes: "The rule of our spiritual life is found in the Bible, which I believe was totally and completely inspired by God." I found particularly refreshing what he said about hell: "The only thing I could say for sure is that hell means separation from God. . . . When it comes to a literal fire, I don't preach it because I'm not sure about it." Compare this view with the harsh pronouncements about sin and punishment offered by evangelicals on the Christian Right and you will appreciate the difference! The Jewish people obviously don't agree with Billy Graham's Christian conviction that Jesus is the son of God who died for our sins. But as Pope John Paul II stresses in his autobiographical work *Crossing the Threshold of Hope,* Judaism is the true religion for the Jewish people, and Catholicism is the true faith for the Catholics. They all will be saved. It took the church a long time to come to this understanding.

      🐾   🐾   🐾

In earlier chapters I have mentioned the Reverend Dr. Robert H. Schuller, whose Sunday services from his Crystal Cathedral in Garden Grove, California, are broadcast all over the world and enjoy a huge audience in the former Soviet Union. He was influenced in his theology by many Jews, the first being Jesus, of course, who he claims is responsible for his salvation. Dr. Schuller also credits the famous psychiatrist Viktor Frankl, author of *Man's Search for Meaning,* as a significant influence in his life. Another person who had a significant impact on Schuller's spiritual development was the famous author and minister, Norman Vincent Peale, who was a pastor at one of the Protestant churches in Syracuse for some years and the purveyor of the concept of positive thinking. Dr. Schuller invited him to preach the first sermon at the new cathedral.

Schuller was brought up in the belief that all people were sinners who had to be saved by God's grace in order to escape the torments of hell. The Reverend Peale expressed quite a different set of ideas. He admonished his audience not to dwell on past sins (going back to the time of Adam), but instead to realize that they are all basically good people who have the potential for good. Due to Peale's considerable influence, Dr. Schuller was able to break away from his more traditional fundamental Christian faith and embrace the broader, more conciliatory view of doing justice to all religions of the world.

Dr. Schuller invited not only speakers from various Protestant denominations, but also Catholic dignitaries (like Bishop Fulton J. Sheen) and Jews, with whom he was able to identify. Is it any wonder, then, that some young Christian fundamentalists who try to convert everyone to their brand of religion explain to me that Dr. Schuller is not really a "Christian"?

Being a convert to the views of Reverend Peale, Dr. Schuller wrote numerous books about the art of positive thinking. In 1992 a highly praised biography of Dr. Schuller was written by James Penner, a television producer and journalist, under the title *Goliath*. I sent Dr. Schuller my autobiography *Once a Doctor* and asked him to make his congregation familiar with it. Mr. Larry Sonnenberg, Dr. Schuller's chief of staff, was kind enough to acknowledge its receipt.

In recent years the Reverend Robert A. Schuller, the elder Schuller's son, has taken over some of the sermons and interviews; I have found him to be as interesting and openminded as his father.

The younger Schuller's latest book bears the title *What Happens to Good People When Bad Things Happen.* This title is no doubt intended to remind readers of Rabbi Harold Kushner's popular volume *When Bad Things Happen to Good People,* published over fifteen years ago. Kushner's son suffered from Progeria, an affliction characterized by the rapid premature aging of the body until death occurs in the early teens—a heartbreaking situation for the patient and family alike. Rabbi Kushner was not able to believe in a God of mercy anymore, especially after this tragedy struck his family. God, Kushner felt, is on our side, but not all-powerful. Human beings have free will and are able to commit bad acts; even God cannot stop them. When tragedy strikes, God does not want to punish us for our sins, and he does not want to test us. God created nature, which has "its own blind laws," and even the creator cannot interfere with its forces. Kushner's book, a *New York Times* reviewer wrote, "presents views at least as plausible as the more common explanations we hear."

Reverend Robert A. Schular's book is very well-written

and most entertaining. He has a very busy and interesting life helping others—a life not always free from tragedy itself. Quite a few years ago, his father and the family were in the Netherlands. The elder Dr. Schuller accidentally hit his head while opening a car door. The blow was so severe that he was hospitalized and in a coma with a subdural hematoma. Blood actually had to be drained from his skull. The brain surgeon and other doctors who treated Schuller in the intensive care unit doubted he would ever recover. But his family and friends kept praying at his bedside until he regained consciousness, made a full recovery, and returned to his active ministry.

People from other religious and nonreligious traditions doubt that Dr. Schuller's recovery would not have taken place if it were not for the many prayers. The Lord gives us temporary pain, according to the younger Dr. Schuller, to spare us from worse afflictions.

In *What Happens to Good People When Bad Things Happen* Dr. Schuller's son talks about the California earthquakes and how people became better for having such a dreadful experience befall them. It taught them what is important and what is not. This strikes me a bit odd. Take, for instance, the people who were killed or maimed in the devastation. What did the experience teach them?

In another part of his book, the young Dr. Schuller tells us that he was sailing "down the coast of the Baja peninsula" when his boat's steering wheel gave out. It was the middle of the night and he was about four hundred miles from the nearest port. Schuller prayed fervently, when suddenly he "saw the glimmer of two lights," a red light next to a green light, which "signals the entrance to a harbor." He was able to manipulate his boat to the nearby harbor, where he found a place to stay overnight and repaired the steering in the morning.

Naturally, we are happy that this good and meritorious gentleman has been saved. Most people in such a dangerous situation might resort to prayer, or at least some intense meditation. Yet it seems that this minister apparently believes that he was able to survive through the power of his prayer. Does that mean that without an ardent prayer a human being could not rely on the help of God to save him or her from destruction?

I have also read the works of the elder Dr. Robert H. Schuller. In recent years, he penned a volume titled *Prayer: My Soul's Adventure with God—A Spiritual Autobiography.* Like most of those who may listen to his Sunday morning messages (whether the listener is a believer or a skeptic), I find it hard to believe that the outcome of his tragic brain surgery in Holland would have been less successful without prayer. I read again about the breast cancer with which his wife, Arvella, was afflicted, requiring her to undergo a mastectomy and follow-up radiation treatments. And I remember the accident to Dr. Schuller's daughter, which required the amputation of one of her legs. Today she is happily married with a family. Neither she nor her father ever lost faith. I did not know about the divorce of the younger Dr. Schuller, however. No doubt these were trying times, indeed, especially for the elder Dr. Schuller and his wife, both of whom were raised at a time when divorce (the infamous "broken marriage") was the rare exception. But I could not believe my eyes when I read the elder Schuller's comment on the breakup of his son's marriage: "It hurt me more to see my only son lose his first wife than it did to see my teenage daughter lose her leg or to see Arvella lose her breast." This statement was surely made as a consequence of the author's having been raised in a strict Protestant tradition.

🐜   🐜   🐜

When scandals rocked other television ministers, Dr. Schuller and his organization remained above the fray. He also kept out of politics and did not become involved with any of the political parties or candidates. Instead, he continued his spiritual message. Once, when Dr. Schuller had noted psychiatrist and concentration camp survivor Dr. Victor Frankl on his program, he asked Dr. Frankl what he considered to be the deepest need of human beings. Without hesitation Frankl replied that the will to meaning is the deepest need of the human soul.

One day in the early 1980s Dr. Schuller was having his friend Dr. Norman Vincent Peale as his guest. The younger Dr. Schuller advised his father to invite Dr. Armand Hammer to come listen to Dr. Peale's message. The elder Schuller remembered that Hammer's father had been one of the founders of the American Communist Party, so he voiced doubt that Dr. Hammer would be interested in listening to Dr. Peale. When his son persisted, Dr. Schuller sat down and wrote Dr. Hammer an invitation. To his surprise, Dr. Hammer phoned to accept the invitation and to comment that he really enjoyed the program.

The elder Schuller was delighted that a friendship soon developed between himself and Dr. Hammer, who had seen the Schuller program in Europe and was anxious for the Russian people to listen to it. Not long thereafter, Dr. Schuller was flown in Dr. Hammer's private jet to the then Soviet Union "with Gorbachev's personal approval." Hammer was so well known and respected in the Soviet state that every person in authority listened to him. Reverend Schuller was interviewed first by "Natalia," the Barbara Walters of Russian television. And from the time of that interview, his program from the Crystal Cathedral has been broadcast every Sunday to a multitude of Russian citizens. When Boris Yeltsin was elected president he invited Schuller to his headquarters and saw to it that the weekly religious television program continued on the air.

      🐾   🐾   🐾

On the last Sunday of 1995 we took note that Dr. Schuller had as his guest the actress Rhonda Fleming, whose sister had died of ovarian cancer some years ago. Ms. Fleming suffered with her sister, but she found a lot of hope and insight in Dr. Schuller's spiritual autobiography. With the help of her Jewish husband, Ms. Fleming built treatment centers for cancer patients, with the care being given free of charge to all who need it. Ms. Fleming had found peace in her life.

The previous week Heather Whitestone, Miss America 1995, was interviewed by Schuller. As a child, she had lost her hearing due to the effects of an antibiotic, but she is able to make herself understood. She, too, never lost faith or hope.

Some readers might justly wonder why I insist on my Jewishness if I claim to gain so much satisfaction from Dr. Schuller's programs and those of other Christian ministers. The answer is quite simple: the basic message is a universal one that most Jews or non-Jews can appreciate.

🐾 🐾 🐾

On one of his programs Reverend Schuller had as his guest civil rights activist and politician Andrew Young, who that particular Sunday morning had inscribed for congregants of the Crystal Cathedral copies of his new book *A Way Out of No Way,* his inspirational memoir. It is a warm, often humorous autobiography that reports on his participation in the often danger-filled civil rights marches with Martin Luther King Jr. It also recounts the severe illness of his beloved wife, Jean. In all his trials and tribulations, and later when he gained recognition by being elected to high office, Young believed that God was at his side. "At each stage of life, God has provided for our needs in every challenging situation." Not many of us can have the same strong faith as Andrew Young; but since early childhood he was interested in Bible study, and after graduation from Howard University he attended Hartford Seminary to study for the ministry.

Andrew Young's hardest task was to convince his father, a respected black dentist, that it was impossible for him to follow in his footsteps and take up dentistry as a profession. His father finally forgave his son for going off to seek his own destiny. In later years Andrew Young served as a member of the U.S. Congress; was elected for two terms as mayor of Atlanta, Georgia; and served as U.S. Ambassador to the United Nations under President Carter. When Young was being sworn in as the U.N. ambassador, President Carter said to Andrew's father, "You must be very proud of your son." According to Andrew Young's book, his father replied, "If he had been a dentist, he really would have been somebody."

It was in March of 1963 that Martin Luther King Jr., made his eloquent "I Have a Dream" speech during a massive civil rights march on Washington, D.C. When asked if the anniversaries of this important date should be celebrated, Andrew Young replied, "Like the Jews have celebrated Passover as their time of understanding of God's deliverance, I expected those Americans whose ancestors were brought to these shores as slaves, artisans, and indentured servants would continue to come back to Washington to celebrate survival and deliverance." There is a common bond between Jews, blacks, whites, and the religions of all nations, who celebrate the important Passover holiday with the Jewish people.

🐾 🐾 🐾

For many years now, and especially since my autobiography was published, I have invited Jews and non-Jews, some of them disabled, to participate in the reading from the Hagadah, describing the exodus of the Jews from Egypt. This meal, which includes readings from the Hebrew text (with English translation), is called Seder and takes place on the eve of Passover. Many Christian sources believe that the Last Supper was held on that night.

11

Other Views of Religion and Judaism

After writing so much on spiritual or religious topics, I expect to hear from some of my more "rational" friends. They will ask, "How can you write so much about things we don't believe in?" All I can say is that I write what I must write. But I like those who call themselves rationalists; my intent is not to antagonize them. In fairness, then, I shall write about one of America's most well-known nonbelievers.

Take, for instance, the late Madalyn Murray O'Hair. I saw her first on the old *Tonight* show with Johnny Carson, where she was taking her seat while the band played "When the Saints Go Marching In." Both the audience and Ms. O'Hair were delighted. I saw her again a few years ago on the old *Donahue* show. There she was appearing for the second time in twenty-five years. The host of the show greeted her by saying: "You have done a lot for the separation of church and state, and God bless you for it!" O'Hair made a thumbs down sign and told the audience that she had read the Bible, didn't like it, and threw it away.

Then Phil Donahue held up the second revised edition of O'Hair's book bearing the title *Why I Am an Atheist.* It is fifty-six pages long, *with an index.* I didn't find out anything more about the author's beliefs from the book than I did by listening to her on the talk show. So, I turned instead to the work titled *My Life without God,* written by one of her sons, who later became a Christian. To tell you the truth, I didn't find out much about his mother from his book.

Actually, William Murray's book says very little about his own conversion, his faith, or his religious convictions; but it describes in more detail Madalyn O'Hair's atheistic views. She was quite anti-Semitic, telling William on one occasion: "Listen kid, the United States of America is nothing more than a fascist slave labor camp run by a handful of 'Jew bankers' in New York City." According to Murray, "Mother was quoted as saying that President Carter was a great aid to the atheist cause because he keeps smiling and putting his foot in his mouth and quoting those idiocies, because the Bible is an idiotic book."

            🐜   🐜   🐜

Several years ago, there appeared a massive anthology by Allan Gould under the title *What Did They Think of the Jews?* In a review of the book, the noted Toronto philosopher Emil Fackenheim had this to say: "Why have so many Gentiles found it necessary to either hate or love Jews, and find it impossible to view them as ordinary folk? I suspect the ultimate reason is the book on account of which the Jews still exist—the Hebrew Bible."

You don't have to be an atheist to become an anti-Semite. Martin Luther, leader of the Protestant Reformation (1483-1546), originally wanted to convert Jews to Christianity by gentle persuasion. He saw that the Catholic popes, bishops, and monks did not treat the Jews well at all. According to Allan Gould, Luther said, "If I had been a Jew and had seen such idiots and blockheads ruling and teaching the Christian religion, I would rather have been a sow than a Christian." But when Luther was unable to convert many Jews to Protestantism, he wrote in *Concerning the Jews and Their Lies*: "What then shall we Christians do with this damned rejected race of Jews? . . . First, their synagogues or churches should be set on fire. . . . Secondly, their homes should likewise be broken down and destroyed. . . . Thirdly, they should be deprived of their prayer books and Talmuds." And it goes on and on. In fairness to Martin Luther it should be pointed out that some writers believe that the quoted essay was not really his work, but written by his adversaries. Let us give Martin Luther the benefit of the doubt.

I have in my possession *Religio Medici,* a small volume by Sir Thomas Browne, who lived from 1605 to 1682. This book about the religion of a physician is, of course, highly recommended as a classic by well-known medical writers. I had intended to read it sometime in its entirety. But then I learned about the following quotations from Browne's book, which were reprinted in Allan Gould's *What Did They Think of the Jews?* "The religion of the Jews is expressly against the Christian. . . . The Jew is obstinate in all fortunes; the persecution of fifteen hundred years hath but confirmed them in their Errour: they have already endured whatsoever may be inflicted, and have suffered in a bad cause, even to the condemnation of their enemies." I no longer plan to read *Religio Medici.*

After writing about the slanted views on the Jewish people by Martin Luther and Sir Thomas Browne, it feels good to discuss Steve Allen's humanistic *Steve Allen on the Bible, Religion, & Morality.* There is no more creative author in the United States than Mr. Allen. He composed about four thousand songs, is an accomplished piano player, was the creator and first host of the *Tonight* show, and (as the reader remembers) was the guest on many panel shows of the fifties, including *What's My Line?* He played the bandleader in the movie *The Benny Goodman Story,* and has written more than forty books.

Coming from an Irish-Catholic background, Steve Allen is not a Catholic anymore, since divorcing his first wife and marrying his present wife, Jayne Meadows. Still, he has debated on friendly terms with priests and other Catholic dignitaries about God, atheism, religion, and the Bible. As a young man he started reading the Gideon Bible in hotel rooms during his various travels; he continued this habit for more than twenty years. The result was his book on the Bible, religion, and morality, published in 1990.

One has to marvel at Steve Allen's knowledge of the Hebrew Scriptures and of the New Testament. He tried to read the Bible with an open mind, using the help of Christian and Jewish biblical scholars. He shows us contradictions in many of the biblical stories and points out the various actions and situations that, from our point of view, have to be considered grossly immoral. Steve Allen is very apologetic about his criticisms and admitted that he had originally intended to publish his book posthumously, but he changed his mind because "an element of urgency had entered the dialogue." This is hard to understand for a non-Christian; Reformed or even conservative Jews do not hesitate to write books critical of scripture.

His original commentaries on biblical subjects and personalities are written by Allen in alphabetical order. I enjoyed especially his chapter on anti-Semitism, in which he offers a personal account. He says that in his third year at a high school "whose student body was largely Jewish" he was cured from the notion that the Jews were generally inferior. He appreciated his new Jewish friends, and found them later to be superior American citizens.

Jewish people will likely find fault with Allen, because he dislikes so many stories of the Old Testament: the story of Abraham, the Book of Ruth, the prophesies of Amos. As a matter of fact, by comparing the vengeful God Jehovah to the God of love in the New Testament, he makes his readers wonder why the majority of Jews still cling to Judaism. As pointed out earlier, the Hebrew Scriptures describe the biblical personalities with all their faults. Yet Judaism evolved from a more primitive outlook to a highly ethical one, as expressed by most of the Psalms, the prophets, the proverbs, and the rabbis in the Talmud and the later chassidic masters.

Be that as it may, Steve Allen's volume was of such enormous interest, and garnered such acclaim, that in 1993 a second volume appeared under the title *More Steve Allen on the Bible, Religion & Morality.* Before I knew that this second volume had appeared, my granddaughter, Sarah, had purchased Steve Allen's *Beloved*

Son: A Story of the Jesus Cults for me at the Dewitt Library book-sale. It seems that in 1971 Allen received a letter from his son Brian, who had joined a religious commune in Seattle, Washington. Brian informed his father that he would not see him or any other member of the Allen family in the future. Still, Steve Allen managed in the ten years between 1971 and the writing of the book in 1982 to visit Brian's religious commune. He interviewed commune members and concerned parents. I am sure that the writing of his book helped ease his grief about losing his son to this cult.

Although he was able, against all odds, to keep in contact with the commune, I am sure that it was very hard for Steve Allen and his family to lose Brian to the Jesus cult. No matter how reasonable their explanations may seem, one never knows how a leader might change or how extreme his views might become. (One need only look at the Jim Jones group or the Branch Davidians who followed David Koresh to see just how extreme such cult-like groups can become.) Any family who loses a son or daughter to a cult deserves our deepest sympathy.

I was amazed to read the following in *Beloved Son*: "Loving one's neighbor is the heart of the Christian message. . . . What made Christianity something special . . . is that it contained the idea of brotherly love not as a vaguely admirable ideal . . . but as a no exceptions, flesh and blood, everyday reality." According to statements of the author, there was no such brotherly love visible in the message of the Hebrew Scriptures, and humankind had to wait for Jesus' appearance to conform to the ideal of loving one's neighbor. In my opinion, this is simply not true! The idea of the "inferiority" of the Old Testament was preached for centuries by the Catholic Church, under Pope John XXIII, until the present Pope John Paul II recognized Judaism as a religion in its own right. While I may disagree with Steve Allen in this matter, nothing here can detract from the fact that we all hope and pray that the relations and communication between son Brian and his loving family should become more healthy and satisfactory in the future.

(One son Steve Allen has never had to worry about is Stephen

Allen Jr., a physician who did his medical residency in general medicine on Long Island and then moved to Upstate New York to practice family medicine. He never felt the urge to follow his famous father on to the stage. Instead, he uses his inherited sense of humor to make patients laugh with his funny stories. On the second floor of his Ithaca home, Dr. Stephen Allen Jr., treats corporate executives, Cornell University faculty, and other professionals. During the day he is an associate dean at the Binghamton Clinical Campus of the State University of New York Health Science Center Medical School. The doctor's face is covered by a greyish beard, but he shows quite a resemblance to his famous father.)

&   &   &

Crossing the Threshold of Hope by Pope John Paul II has been out for a while now and has enjoyed best-seller status on many published lists. John Paul has known and loved the Jewish people since he went to elementary school in his Polish hometown of Wadowice, where at least a fourth of the pupils in his class were Jewish. The pope gives special mention to one of his friends, Jerzy Kluger, a man who survived the Holocaust and is still in constant contact with the pontiff. It was Jerzy Kluger who asked John Paul to honor with a memorial plaque the place where the synagogue at Wadowice had stood. The synagogue was destroyed by the Nazis. It was a very emotional experience for Kluger, who visited his hometown for the first time in fifty years. All the members of his family who had remained in that small town died at Auschwitz. At the unveiling of the plaque, Jerzy Kluger read to his fellow citizens a personal note from his friend the pope expressing the pontiff's solidarity and "spiritual union on the occasion of such an important event."

When the pope's book was reviewed by the *New York Times,* the reviewer, Gustav Niebuhr, could not agree with the theological concepts of the pope, just as I—a Jew—cannot see eye to eye with Catholic doctrine. But I was very pleased to see that the *Times* reviewer found John Paul's recollection of his childhood in

Wadowice one of the warmest parts of the autobiography. He felt that this showed the goodness of the pope more than any chapter could.

The turning point for the Catholic Church came with the declaration *Nostra Aetate,* which also is Pope John Paul II's declaration: "The Church of Christ . . . recognizes that . . . the origins of the Church's faith and election are already found in the patriarchs, Moses, and the prophets. . . . Therefore, since the spiritual patrimony common to Christians and Jews is so great, this Sacred Council . . . promotes a mutual respect, which can be obtained . . . through biblical study and fraternal discussion." When talking about Judaism the pope speaks of the religion closest "to our own—that of the people of God of the Old Testament."

🜚　🜚　🜚

David LaRocco, one of my granddaughter's friends, attended the Newhouse School of Communications at Syracuse University. Aside from journalism, he took Italian during his last semester and planned to spend the following semester as an exchange student in Italy. Sarah and David met when he attended a Simon Weisenthal lecture at Syracuse University's Schine Auditorium with a Jewish friend. David read my *Once a Doctor* and has seen parts of the present book in manuscript form. He hoped to have an audience with Pope John Paul II and present him with an autographed copy of my autobiography. David also planned to give an inscribed copy of my book to Rome's Chief Rabbi, Elio Toaff, head of Rome's fifteen thousand member Jewish community. It was in 1986 when Pope John Paul II visited Chief Rabbi Toaff and attended a service with him at the Rome synagogue, the first time in history that a pope ever attended a Jewish service.

🜚　🜚　🜚

Another book I had occasion to read and enjoy was *The Wellness Prescription,* written by Jewish physician Dr. Edward A. Taub and published in 1994. Soon after it came out, I saw the author on

Reverend Schuller's weekly program from the Crystal Cathedral, where Dr. Taub had just autographed copies of his new volume. He spoke as a guest of his old friend Dr. Schuller, whose sermons he had listened to since the assassination of President John F. Kennedy. Dr. Taub worked at that time as a resident at one of the hospitals "across the road" from Schuller's church.

The Wellness Prescription speaks to readers about diet, exercise, sleep, and the need for medication; but in addition to these, Dr. Taub also goes into details about the three addictions that rob us of our energy: addictions to alcohol, caffeine, and tobacco. Most of all, he dares—as no other book has—to talk about the soul. Dr. Taub frequently cites *Care of the Soul* by Thomas Moore, a former Catholic monk and psychotherapist. Citing numerous case studies, Dr. Taub shows us that many of his patients would never have been healed had he not talked with them about love, forgiveness, helping others, and the need for a spiritual outlook—things you cannot find in an ordinary textbook on medicine.

                                             ❦   ❦   ❦

I would like to conclude this chapter by returning to Joseph Telushkin's book *Jewish Wisdom,* to my mind one of the most comprehensive works ever written on Judaism by anyone. No doubt those from other religions will continue in their slanted views about the Jewish people and their teachings. You will recall that I was impressed with his work titled *The Nine Questions People Ask about Judaism,* coauthored with Dennis Prager, and with his fascinating work titled *Jewish Literacy: The Most Important Things to Know about the Jewish Religion, Its People, and Its History.*

Telushkin's *Jewish Literacy* is most notable because, not all that long ago, my grandson, Maurice, attended a course titled "Basic Judaism" at Cortland State University taught by Dr. Suzanne Stewart. In preparing an extensive paper for the class, Maurice consulted Telushkin's *Jewish Literacy* a great deal. (When Dr. Stewart received from me a copy of *Once a Doctor,* she invited me to talk with her class about the conditions in Nazi Germany that led to the Holocaust. Dr. Stewart comes from a family of Holocaust survivors. She grew up in Germany and attended school there.)

Joseph Telushkin's *Jewish Wisdom* is a companion work to Francine Klagbrun's *Voices of Wisdom: Jewish Ideals and Ethics for Everyday Living,* from which he quotes freely (with her permission). The powerful quote from Leviticus "Do not stand idly by while your neighbor's blood is shed" would have been a tremendous help in preventing the persecutions of the Middle Ages and the horrors of the Nazis during the thirties and forties had the nations of the world only paid attention to it. Remember what Rabbi Hillel said to the heathen who asked to be converted to Judaism while standing on one foot: "What is hateful to you, do not do to your neighbor; this is the whole of the Torah. The rest is commentary, now go and study."

Although Telushkin makes clear that for Judaism marriage is a sacred institution, he makes it abundantly clear that divorce is preferable to continuing in a marriage in which there are irreconcilable differences. I was not surprised, then, when on July 30, 1994, my daughter, Joan, and her husband, Mel, became legally separated after twenty-eight years of marriage. They remain on very friendly terms, and Joan and the children have lived with me since the separation.

When one reads in the Book of Exodus "Honor your father and mother," and in Leviticus that "You shall rise before the aged and show deference to the old," one has to think of the pronouncements of some youth groups in history: "Never trust anyone over thirty!" Is it any wonder, then, that so many people despise the Jews for their "old fashioned" views, which they continue to teach from one generation to the next? We also learn from Leviticus, as quoted in *Jewish Wisdom,* "Do not go about as a talebearer among your people." In the work titled *Ethics of the Fathers* we find this gem: "Who is rich? One who is happy with what he has." I recall once recounting this dictum to some business people. They looked at me as though I had said something utterly ridiculous.

12

Personal Convictions

I have had in my library since about 1980 a book by Dr. Carl Sagan titled *Cosmos*. The book was given to me by my friend Betty Gould with her thanks for my medical care of her brain-injured and disabled son, Clifford, who also inscribed it for me. (When Betty died quite some time ago, Clifford stayed for a while at the home of his older brother, Rick. The time and attention needed to take care of his brother placed Rick's job in jeopardy, so he made arrangements for Clifford to stay at a supervised halfway house. Even though Rick was roundly criticized by friends and relatives for taking this action, I suspect it was for the best. I have never seen Clifford so well-mannered or better able to communicate than he is now.)

Carl Sagan's book *Cosmos* was the inspiration for a popular series of TV programs watched by millions of people, and the book was on the best-seller list for a very long time. Eventually it appeared in paperback. Sagan was often asked to do guest appearances on various talk shows and news programs dealing with science topics. He was even a frequent guest on Johnny Carson's *Tonight* show. Ithaca, New York, the home of Cornell University, where Dr. Sagan was a member of the astrophysics faculty, should be proud to have had this eminent scientist as one of its leading citizens. Unlike my grandchildren who have taken astronomy courses, I lack sufficient knowledge about the movement of the stars. But my wife, Herta, always found time to sit patiently and watch as Dr. Sagan explained the movements of the planets and unlocked the secrets of the universe for his viewers.

Most of the critics of *Cosmos* come from the Christian fundamentalist camp, while a few ultra-Orthodox Jews were also perturbed that the scientist's account of the universe did not conform to the biblical creation story. There should be no problem, however, since the validity of the Bible should not stand or fall with the literal interpretation of the Scriptures.

I just recently rediscovered, tucked away in my paperback edition of *God and the Astronomers* by astrophysicist Robert Jastrow, a short letter from the editor of the *New York Times* dated 1981. The writer tells us that in 1876 Darwin received a pamphlet from a rabbi in Radom, Poland, who explained to the scientist that the theory of evolution was consistent with the Old Testament account of creation.

But there have always been critical voices. I remember an article written in *Moment* magazine by Marc Gellman in 1981 under the title "Sagan the Pagan." There was a letter of response by a reader in the very next issue. Although I am neither a theologian nor a philosopher, I can understand Gellman's point. He feels that for Sagan the myths of the old Greeks or from old Mexico are comparable to the Hebrew Bible or to the Jewish-Christian tradition. For the Jewish people this Bible is our biography and history, teaching us and all humankind some very basic laws and commandments, seeking to lead us into a messianic future. With this in mind, I found myself rereading the following passage in Deuteronomy: "For this commandment which I command you this day is not too hard for you, nor too remote. It is not in heaven. . . . Nor is it beyond the sea. . . . No, it is very near to you, in your mouth and in your heart, and you can do it."

In reading *Cosmos* and Dr. Sagan's other books, I am

reminded of the conversation between Rabbi Joshua and the Emperor Trajan. When the emperor demanded to see God, the rabbi replied, "First, you must attempt to look at one of his creations." He then asked the emperor to look at the sun. When the emperor replied that he couldn't do this, because the sun's light "dazzles me," Rabbi Joshua replied: "You are unable to look at one of his creations? How can you expect to see the Creator? It would annihilate you."

Some time ago, not long after Sagan's *Shadows of Forgotten Ancestors* was published, in collaboration with his wife, Ann Drujan, they appeared on the popular *Regis and Kathie Lee* talk show. Kathie Lee asked Dr. Sagan if he believed in God. The famous scientist gave her his pat answer: "It depends, what kind of a God?"

"Well," Kathie Lee replied, "I believe in a God who counts every hair on my scalp."

Although I empathize with Kathie Lee's comments and her delightful book *I Can't Believe I Said That,* I must agree with Dr. Sagan's reply especially when thinking of the Christian Right, whose leaders only recognize their own brand of fundamentalist religion.

In *Shadows of Forgotten Ancestors* Sagan and Drujan agree with the Darwinian idea that monkeys and apes are our closest relatives. According to the philosopher John Dewey, the human memory distinguishes us from the other animals. Other philosophers, like René Descartes, believed that language makes us different from other animal species. But this is not true, according to the Sagan and Drujan. There are many instances of sign language and use of gestures among the apes and other higher animals. Chimpanzees also laugh and smile a lot say the authors. Though I am not a scientist, I cannot forget the story I learned while growing up in Germany. Little Max comes home from school one day and asks his father whether it's true what they learned in school—that "we are descended from the apes." The father, visibly angered, replies, "Maybe you, but not me!"

People sometimes insist on the fact of their animal nature,

especially when they are accused of a crime. Sigmund Freud calls this animal nature the *id,* which is controlled by our *superego,* our conscience. Animals, no matter how smart they are or loving to each other they may be, have no conscience. One need only think of the canine companions of the evil S.S. men in the concentration camps to realize this. The S.S. loved their big dogs. These animals would obediently tear their hapless victims to shreds whenever their "masters" demanded. Dennis Overbye, in a *Time* essay written in April of 1993, summed it up for me in his article titled "The Fact that Science Cannot Find Any Purpose to the Universe Does Not Mean There Is Not One." *Shadows of Forgotten Ancestors* is a beautifully written and well-documented book but it didn't tell me how I should live my life. I have a right to know at my age. So, I purchased Carl Sagan's book *The Pale Blue Dot* in the hope that possibly this book would hold the answer.

The Pale Blue Dot is, of course, our Earth. In addition to the universe, our galaxy, and all the various planets in our solar system, we cannot forget the little planet we live on. "I don't for a moment propose that the Earth is a disposable planet, and we have to put enormous efforts into making sure we don't mess up down here. . . . The Earth is the only world known so far to harbor life. . . . It has been said that astronomy is a humbling and character-building experience. . . . To me, it underscores our responsibility to deal more kindly with one another, and to preserve and cherish the pale blue dot, the only home we've ever known."

Yet, toward the end of his beautifully illustrated book this internationally known scientist refers to the psychologist-philosopher William James, who called religion a "feeling of being in the Universe." And to this Dr. Sagan responds: "If, in considering James's definition, we mean the real Universe, then we have no true religion yet. That is for another time, when . . . we are acclimatized to other worlds and they to us, when we are spreading to the stars." I cannot wait that long! Now that I am in my eighties, I would like to know right now what to do with my life. Everyone can find his/her own tradition, what purpose there may be in life every day of the year, as long as he/she does not try to force that particular faith on someone else.

      🐾   🐾   🐾

I found myself rereading Kathie Lee Gifford's *I Can't Believe I Said That.* Hers is an inspirational book—much more so than some of our deep theological dissertations.

    Kathie Lee's father was of mixed heritage. He had a Jewish father and a Christian mother, a woman who brought him up in the Christian faith. His name was Aaron Leon Epstein. When he was about ten, he was on his way to his Episcopal Church in Annapolis, Maryland, when a gang of young boys threw rocks at him and started to yell "Christ-killer! Christ-killer!" This event took place in the mid 1930s, and Kathie Lee's father was never able to forget it.

    Neither did his daughter. As a matter of fact, she was reminded of her maiden name when she was hired in May of 1977 for a large part in a Ralph Edwards television show and was asked by a producer with a skeptical smirk how she would feel about changing the name Epstein? The producer didn't think it was especially lyrical. At that time she was married to the fundamentalist Christian composer and conductor Paul Johnson. They had agreed to keep their names separate at the time of their marriage.

    Kathie Lee's parents consider themselves born-again Christians, but they have never identified with the Christian Right. They, as well as their daughter, became interested in their Christian faith through the help of the Reverend Billy Graham. Apparently, she also considers herself a Hebrew Christian. I think that she wants to come to grips with her Jewish heritage though she never tries to convert anybody to her brand of faith. Although she has changed the direction of her religious outlook several times, Kathie Lee's deep biblical faith has never left her.

    Kathie Lee has suffered many trials and tribulations: Her

sister Michie almost died during the surgical removal of her colon. And Michie's young daughter, Shannon, had to have open-heart surgery due to pulmonary stenosis, but she survived. Kathie Lee herself was married to Paul Johnson for six years in a very unhappy marriage, which finally ended in divorce. As I understand from Kathie Lee's book, she was thrilled with Paul's deeply Christian religious compositions, and she felt they were in love with each other, but when her secular career began to take off, they grew more and more apart. Strangely enough, she never blames him for anything. They remain friends.

Gradually, she moved away from her rigid Christian fundamentalist attitudes and developed her more realistic faith. Actually Kathie Lee never believed in the Christian Right's radical religious views. When she was quite young she had been advised by Anita Bryant to get an education at Oral Roberts University, but after investigating it Kathie Lee just couldn't believe in the things that were taught there, and the school didn't have classes in the areas that interested her. Later on Kathie Lee and sister Michie paid a visit to Tammy Bakker, but all the Bakkers seemed interested in was their desire to build up their religious empire. In addition, there was a good bit of faith healing with these groups—something Kathie Lee abhors.

It was the biggest event in Kathie Lee's life when she fell in love with the famous sports personality Frank Gifford. There was, of course, quite a difference in their ages, and Frank already had a grown family. While he was not thrilled with the idea of starting a new family, he loved and respected Kathie Lee and felt happy for her when she became pregnant with their son, Cody. Frank was present at all the Lamaze classes and he participated in all the birth procedures. He was a very proud father. The birth of a son at his age was quite an experience for Frank.

Both Frank and Kathie Lee decided in 1991 that Cody should have a little brother or sister. In July of 1992 Kathie's pregnancy test came back positive. Unfortunately, while on vacation in Colorado, she suffered a miscarriage when she was just seven weeks pregnant. At a Vail, Colorado, hospital the gynecologist consoled her by explaining that the baby might not have been healthy and that she could definitely have more children. When Frank asked the doctor how he should handle paying for his services, the doctor mentioned that there was no charge since he was glad to be of help in honor of his mother, who had been a big fan of Frank's. When Frank wanted to give a donation to charity in the name of the doctor's mother, the physician said something that Kathie Lee claims she now has written on her heart forever: "Just do something kind for someone, and tell them to pass it on." She never forgot, and soon she was pregnant with a healthy baby girl, whom they named Cassidy.

To conclude, I would like to quote from Kathie Lee's own words, expressing her spiritual convictions: "God didn't bless me with success so that I could eat caviar every day. Not a day goes by that the Lord doesn't etch in my heart the passages of Scripture I grew up with: 'What does it profit a man if he gains the whole world but loses his very soul?' [and] 'To whom much is given much is required . . .' [and] 'Don't store your treasures on earth, for where your treasure is your heart can be found, too.'

. . . I feel guilty that my plate is overflowing when millions of American workers and executives have lost their jobs and careers. It isn't fair. It breaks my heart that millions of children go to bed hungry and that others have parents who ignore or abuse them. Charity allows my conscience to coexist with my embarrassment of riches; being a light for the Lord allows me to help fill the void in us that only a spiritual bond can fill."

My secular humanist friends will probably object to these quotations. But Kathie Lee's statements are completely in line with her upbringing and her spiritual beliefs. I understand her, and I also understand my secular friends.

13

Survivors Remembered

At this juncture, I have to mention a letter I received after much delay and waiting. It was sent to me from Survivors of the Shoah: Visual History Foundation. Its chairman is the Hollywood producer Steven Spielberg. You will recall that Spielberg produced and directed the acclaimed film *Schindler's List,* describing the life of a righteous gentile who risked his own life to save a great many Jews from the hands of the Nazis. Shoah is the Hebrew word for the Holocaust. For many years after the persecutions and the Holocaust the majority of survivors were too numb to write about their terrible experiences. And now, most of the survivors have died or are quite old. Spielberg's goal is to conduct interviews with as many survivors as possible "throughout the world, assuring that future generations never forget what happened."

The letter mentioned that a local coordinator would conduct the interview with me at my home. I was to receive a videotape of my interview, which, the letter stated, "we hope will be a meaningful addition to your family library." This will preserve my testimony in its complete and unedited form. All these videotape accounts will be made available to the Holocaust Museum in Washington, D.C., as well as the Simon Wiesenthal Center in California, the Museum of Jewish Heritage in New York, the Fortunoff Video Archive for Holocaust Testimonies at Yale University, and the Yad Vashem in Israel. Here is the text of the letter that I was sent by Survivors of the Shoah:

29 August 1996

Dear Mr. Hartmann,

In sharing your personal testimony as a survivor of the Holocaust, you have granted generations the opportunity to experience a personal connection with history.

Your interview will be carefully preserved as an important part of the most comprehensive library of testimonies ever collected. Far into the future, people will be able to see a face, hear a voice, and observe a life, so that they may listen and learn, and always remember.

Thank you for your invaluable contribution, your strength, and your generosity of spirit.

All my best,

Steven Spielberg
Chairman

The letter was accompanied by a brief questionnaire asking for some pre-interview information and a flyer explaining what would happen to the videotapes once they were collected.

So Generations Never Forget . . . What So Few Lived to Tell, Survivors of the Shoah Visual History Foundation, founded and chaired by Steven Spielberg, is a nonprofit organization seeking Holocaust survivors throughout the world who are interested in recording their eyewitness testimony on videotape. Our goal over the next few years is to create a permanent record of survivors' personal experiences before, during, and after the Holocaust. Survivors who participate will receive a video copy of their testimony. By sharing these stories firsthand, survivors play a vital role in making sure that one of the most devastating events in human history is never forgotten.

The archive testimonies will be made available to museums and nonprofit organizations for historical research and other educational purposes. Each testimony is a legacy for children, grandchildren, and generations to follow. These testimonies honor the memory of those who will never be heard.

If this good news were not enough, Dr. Dena Mandel, who teaches a "Literature of the Holocaust" class at Le Moyne College, invited me to speak to her students in the near future. As usual, the talk would be followed by a question-and-answer period. I had talked on prior occasions at Dr. John Glennon's general religion class and to Dr. Susan Bordo's philosophy students at the same college.

🐿 🐿 🐿

Not long after all of this good news came my way, I received in the mail a much awaited volume, Rabbi Steven L. Jacobs's work titled *Rethinking Jewish Faith: The Child of a Survivor Responds*. This small volume is so important to all Jewish people who grapple with their Jewish identity, as well as to Christians, other religious traditions, and even agnostics. Rabbi Jacobs's father was able to escape Nazi Germany in December 1939. The author was later born in Baltimore, Maryland, in 1947. More than one hundred fifty members of the Jacobs family were murdered by the Third Reich. While Rabbi Jacobs's father was brought up a German Orthodox Jew, his orthodoxy died in the camps. Steven decided early that Judaism and Jewish learning would become his life's goal. He is now rabbi of Temple B'nai Sholom of Huntsville, Alabama, and he teaches Jewish studies at various universities in his area. But he never forgets about the Shoah and the meaning of it all. He does not believe any more in a God who is "protective of His or Her human children." He or She was not able or willing to destroy the evil forces during the years between 1939 and 1945. The author cannot believe in the authoritative God of the Torah, but in the interpretation of the Torah and the responses of the Jewish people in each and every generation. He discusses prayer, the commandments, and our cooperation with the Christian and other communities after the Shoah. We all have to work together so that the Nazi evil will not be repeated anywhere in the world.

I sent my review of Rabbi Jacobs's *Rethinking Jewish Faith* to the *Syracuse Jewish Observer* in the hope that they would publish it, in spite of the fact that they get more and more communications from readers than ever before. These comments and reactions are wonderful, but the space available for them is limited. (We in the Jewish community are very proud of our *Observer*, which is read by Jews and non-Jews alike. It is bigger and more informative than most Jewish papers in the United States, regardless of the size of the population served. The editor for many years has been Mollie Leitzes Collins, and her editorial assistant is Deborah A. Wallace.)

♠   ♠   ♠

During my broad range of reading in various subject areas, I chanced upon the newest reprint of Paul Kurtz's *Living without Religion: Eupraxsophy*. The reader will recall that in addition to being president of Prometheus Books (my publisher), Kurtz is also professor emeritus of philosophy at the State University of New York at Buffalo and editor of *Free Inquiry* magazine.

According to Kurtz, humanism is not a religion, and he considers himself a secular humanist. In order to distinguish his humanist beliefs and practices from those of traditional religions, he has coined the term *eupraxsophy*, which means not only the love of wisdom but the practice of wisdom as well. As he puts it, "It draws from the wells of philosophy, ethics, and science. . . . It involves . . . a set of normative ideas, by which we may live." One of the questions he raises concerns the traditional theist and the search for the good life: "Does [theism] contribute to a better life than humanist eupraxsophies?" Unfortunately, as the author claims, orthodox religious beliefs have dogmas that cannot be scrutinized or questioned, and here is where humanism enters with its eupraxsophy.

I feel somewhat ill at ease discussing this well-written book. I am neither a trained philosopher nor a scientist. But it seems clear to me that the majority of people who are looking for the good life are not able to understand humanist writing since this majority is not peopled with philosophers either. However, they have been able to comprehend their Sunday school lessons. As I pointed out before, my own Jewish tradition doesn't stand or fall on the literal interpretation of the Bible. When I discussed Prager and Telushkin's *Nine Questions People Ask about Judaism* I pointed out that even an atheist is considered a Jew as long as he or she observes the commandments. And these laws and commandments are the finest and most humanistic anywhere in the world!

In this connection I remind my readers of a quotation I used before from a *Free Inquiry* symposium held in Michigan in April of 1985. The contents of the symposium were printed by Prometheus Books under the title *Jesus in History and Myth.* The quote is by the Christian theologian John Hicks: "I do not seek to convert people of the other great religions to Christianity, though I would be very happy if I could convert secular humanists to any one of the great world religions."

At the beginning of *Living without Religion* Paul Kurtz thanks, among others, the famous humanist philosopher Sidney Hook for his valuable suggestions. Hook considered himself an agnostic, but, as the reader will recall, shortly before his departure from this earth, he was interviewed by *Commentary* editor Norman Podhoretz. In that interview we learn that Hook was educated in an Orthodox Jewish environment, which didn't mean very much to him. In the later years of his life, however, he regretted the lack of a really deep Jewish education with its stress on the Sabbath and the meaning of the Jewish holidays, as well as the knowledge to answer the misguided anti-Semitic critics. After that interview it seems to me impossible to call Sidney Hook a "secular" humanist anymore.

It was way back in 1974 when I received from the *Humanist* magazine (edited at the time by Paul Kurtz) a copy of the *Humanist Manifestos I and II*. In addition, I was sent a complimentary copy of the paperback edition of Kurtz's work titled *The Humanist Alternative*. In his preface Kurtz says, "The term Humanism has been used in many senses. There are scientific, religious, atheistic, and ethical Humanists." When reviewing the second Humanist Manifesto one notes that it is signed by quite a few religiously prominent Jews such as Joseph L. Blau, Mordecai M. Kaplan, and Sol Gordon. Among the frequent speakers at *Free Inquiry* sessions have been Ellis Rivkin, a professor at Hebrew Union College and author of *The Shaping of Jewish History* and *What Crucified Jesus?* Is it right, I ask (although I have no right to do so), to declare all of these loyal, highly educated people second-class humanists just because they are not secular?

Right in front of me I have a most important book titled *Finding God: Ten Jewish Responses* by Rifat Sonsino and Daniel B. Syme. It tells us about God in the Bible, in rabbinical literature, in philosophy, in the mysticism of Luria, in the pantheism of Spinoza, in the philosophy of Martin Buber, in the theism of Milton Steinberg, in the religious reconstructionism of Mordecai Kaplan, and in the humanism of Erich Fromm. Many Conservative or Reformed Jews have their spiritual fulfillment in a combination of all of these various Jewish responses. Martin Buber, one of the greatest humanists of all time, carried on a dialogue with God all of his life. Erich Fromm grew up in Germany and studied Judaism there with noted scholars, until he emigrated to the United States in 1934. He was a psychoanalyst and a social psychologist. But all over the world he has been considered the prototype of a humanist.

Top: Maurice Raichelson (grandson), *left*: Joan Raichelson Hartmann (daughter),
right: Sarah Hartmann Klein (granddaughter), *center:* Heinz Hartmann.

Maurice joins his grandfather as they celebrate Maurice's graduation from Syracuse University (1997).

Sarah with her future husband, Lawrence Klein, at their engagement party (1997).

Heinz Hartmann with son, Michael, at the Jewish Home of Central New York.

Michael Hartmann with Ms. Eleene Seeber, his valued caretaker.

This is what he writes about the Bible: "The Bible is an extraordinary book, expressing many norms and principles that have maintained their validity throughout thousands of years. It . . . has proclaimed a vision of men that is still valid and awaiting realization." I never considered Erich Fromm a "secular" humanist, and I don't believe that the reader will, especially after Fromm has told us about his credo in *You Shall Be as Gods* and his several other books. I am grateful, of course, to Paul Kurtz for his *Living without Religion.* It gave me a chance to think about these important topics.

14

More on the Health Front

One morning before breakfast, Terry from Metpath Laboratories arrived on schedule to draw blood from me for my monthly cholesterol (both the good HDL type and the bad LDL type) and triglyceride check, as well as the liver function tests. The following morning I would receive the test results over the telephone from the Metpath coordinator, who will then see to it that I get a written report within the next few days. The day I receive the results they are immediately faxed to Dr. Lance Gould in Houston and to Dr. Kronenberg here in Syracuse. Joan will speak to Dr. Gould once the test results are sent, and Dr. Gould will confer with Dr. Kronenberg before my appointment with the latter by the end of the week. It is all a very synchronized process to maintain my health.

As I mentioned earlier, I decided not to have heart bypass surgery, electing instead to be placed under the care of cardiologist Dr. Lance Gould, one of the foremost researchers in coronary reversal therapy designed to correct the coronary artery blockage through diet and some medication. His program recommends a very low-fat, high-protein diet. These nutrients are obtained from low-fat dairy products, though Dr.

Gould does occasionally permit a bit of turkey or fish. I am so accustomed to the complete vegetarian diet that I rarely deviate. I keep my weight down and exercise regularly when I feel up to it.

Medically, I continue the daily children's aspirin. I take a daily multiple vitamin tablet, as well as high doses of vitamin C, vitamin E, and beta carotene. My blood pressure is completely controlled, but I continue on my Vasotec (5 mg) prescription as a precaution. As the main cholesterol-lowering drug, Dr. Gould prescribed Zocor (10mg daily). He wants to see my cholesterol reduced to below 140, but when we received the latest lab test results a month ago, my reading was 113. This permitted him to cut the Zocor down to 5mg per day.

I still continue to take Isordil (40 mg four times per day) to prevent angina, and Dr. Gould added two Norvasc tablets (5 mg) to my morning regimen. I am permitted to take one Nitrostat tablet (1/200 g) sublingually when needed for chest discomfort, but lately I have not had to use them very often. The Isordil is given one hour before a meal and at least two hours after the preceding meal, while other medications have to be split in two and are administered twice daily.

It might seem that most of my time is taken up with medications, but this is not so. My main task remains writing. When Sarah was still living with us she was very conscientious in helping me. From time to time, a new book would come out pertaining to some aspect of my life experience and I would have to read it before continuing on with my work. She would see that I had a copy of whatever I needed. I also try to keep up with medical literature.

My daughter, Joan, and her family live with me at my home. They help me with my special diet, getting my medications from the pharmacy, and answering all the various telephone calls I receive. Until they departed for school and later left home to begin their own independent lives, my grandchildren lived with me and were a considerable help as well.

Sarah has graduated college, receiving her bachelors degree, with honors, in psychology from Le Moyne College.

She had planned to pursue postgraduate work at Syracuse University, but in order to do that she needed to find work, a job at which her psychology training would be of help. She found such a position with a nationally recognized insurance carrier. She contacts clients all over the country and enjoys the experience she is gaining. Recently, she married Lawrence Klein and they now reside in New York City, where Sarah's postgraduate plans have shifted to New York University.

My grandson, Maurice, attended Syracuse University, where he received his bachelors degree in Transportation Distribution Management in 1997. He, too, is now living in New York City where he works for a major bus tour company.

🐜 🐜 🐜

In order to make the most of my time, I need to keep a good watch. I need to know the time if I am to take my various medications and to determine the interval between the dosages and my next meal. I also take my pulse before exercising on my stationary bicycle or my rowing machine. I still have my old dependable Wittnauer watch, now more than fifty years old and purchased while I was still practicing medicine in Tully, New York, so many years ago. In an effort to be a bit more modern, I tried some automatic watches, which function not by winding but by the movement of my hand, but they never felt quite right.

Nearly thirty-five years ago, now, I was fortunate enough to purchase a Rolex, which was at the time the official time keeper for the Olympic games. It was quite a timepiece—worn by famous people throughout the world. Unable to afford the really expensive style, I purchased a stainless steel model for a fraction of what the gold watches were selling for. Since the cost of repairing my beautiful Rolex forced me to place it in a drawer, I have relied on a Seiko quartz timepiece. I had originally intended to purchase one when my former son-in-law, Mel, remembered that he had given an identical wristwatch to Maurice, but my grandson preferred sports watches. Mel asked Maurice to find the watch and give it to me. I have worn the timepiece ever since. It helps me get through my day and to keep up with my schedule of writing and medications.

         🐜   🐜   🐜

When I saw my internist Dr. Kronenberg for my regularly scheduled appointment, he had received a good report from Dr. Gould. Aside from the good lab reports, Dr. Kronenberg found that I was also physically much better. Due to the Isordil and the two tablets of Norvasc, I have hardly ever had to resort to my Nitrostat, and this made Dr. Kronenberg feel that my angina was more stable.

But while I am on a strict regimen of medications (some of them in several doses during the day), special meals, and required rest periods, I never fail to make time to write.

15

Enriched by Memories
and Dear Friends, Old and New

In the recent past I gave a talk before Professor Dena Mandel's "Literature of the Holocaust" class at Le Moyne College. I am happy to say that the small classroom was filled to capacity, not only with those who registered for the class, but by visiting students as well. My granddaughter, Sarah, gave a short introduction and then I spoke for about fifteen minutes on the topic of my book *Once a Doctor*, reading to them about my general and medical education, the terror of "Crystal Night," my incarceration at Buchenwald, and on anti-Semitism in the United States.

In the question-and-answer period that followed, only a few of the questions could be discussed; the time just flew by so fast. The students wanted to know if I ever regretted the fact that I was born Jewish. Of course not! I could never have been anything else. But I have the deepest respect for believers of any other religious or nonreligious traditions, as long as they don't enforce their point of view on others.

It is difficult to say whether any specific event of the Holocaust sticks out more in my mind than any other. Naturally the Buchenwald Concentration Camp will be etched in my memory forever. There was always the wondering: Would we get out alive? Would we see our loved ones again? But there are other embedded memories as well: thinking of our loved ones after their disappearance in the Holocaust, getting only partial reports from the Red Cross or the Jewish organizations. Those fearful times cannot be erased from our minds, even decades later.

I had written in my previous book about anti-Semitism in America. I discussed this with the students at the Le Moyne College class. So many of my well-meaning friends concluded from their copies of the New Testament that a Jew who does not believe in the fundamentalist Christian faith cannot be saved or go to heaven. Unlike the vitriol of the hate groups, this is a more insidious form of anti-Semitism.

I encouraged the students to communicate with me, and I promised to answer them, as I always do. I enjoyed my reading at Le Moyne College immensely and afterward I received a beautiful "thank you" letter from Professor Mandel, accompanied by a gift of appreciation—a book written by George L. Mosse titled *German Jews Beyond Judaism*. Mosse, who also is an immigrant from Nazi Germany, is Weinstein Bascom Professor of History at the University of Wisconsin-Madison. Sadly, as Mosse's book shows us, the majority of German Jews had abandoned Judaism, and they tried to prove, even under the Nazi regime, how deeply rooted they were in German culture. What a wasted effort that was! Many of the wealthier Jews could instead have escaped Hitler's grip before the most terrible and restrictive laws had taken effect. This could have permitted them to concentrate on the eternal question of their destiny as Jews.

🐜   🐜   🐜

It is hard to believe yet another year has gone by so fast. Soon we will be celebrating the first Passover Seder night, the holiday celebrated by the majority of the Jewish community, and now also by many Christian churches. For many years I had been reading the story of the Exodus from Egypt in Hebrew and English to family and invited Jewish and non-Jewish friends, punctuated by the traditional songs and accompanied by Sarah on the piano. Sarah's friend Elise Shefrin has always been helpful in preparing the holiday dinner for all of us. But this year would be different. Since I am participating in the reversal therapy I am on a very strict diet, one that would not be satisfactory for any of the regularly invited guests. So I held a shorter Seder just for the immediate family. (Our good friend Roz Sagar, who for many years had joined us with her son, Michael, in our Passover celebration, attended the community Seder at Temple Society of Concord on this occasion. She sat at the same table as Dr. Marsha Snyder, another good friend whom she met in our house on many New Year's evenings. Marsha, who has a very busy practice, is never too tired to discuss with us any problems I might be having during my coronary treatment.)

My grandson, Maurice, asked the four questions, and Sarah played the traditional songs on the piano. I had the reversal diet, while Joan prepared a more elaborate meal for herself and the others. Maurice had invited as guests at the Seder table three high school friends: Chris O'Leary, Kenny Porter, and Sean Griffin (all have graduated from college now).

As the days passed before the holiday, I received quite a few letters of appreciation from students who were present at my Le Moyne College lecture the previous April (1995). They thanked me for my reading and for the discussion that followed, which I enjoyed as much as they had. One of the young men asked if I had treated many German Americans after the war and if it was awkward for me to take care of them. I treated many German-American families, none of whom had anything to do with the Nazi regime. They had confidence in me, and my only task (as always) was to find the best manner of treatment for them. I answered every letter, as I said I would. I reminded them to communicate with me again after they had read my earlier autobiography.

Naturally, I expect to hear from the students about their

opinion regarding the Covenant and the Jewish people. Actually, I don't worry about that. You see, Le Moyne College has been rated one of the best colleges in the United States for years. This strictly Jesuit college employs as teachers (aside form Catholic priests) professors of various Protestant denominations as well as those of the Jewish faith.

Along with the students' letters I received a message from the pope! Well, actually one of his emissaries. I had mentioned earlier that Sarah's friend David LaRocco had planned to give an autographed copy of my *Once a Doctor* to the Vatican while he was studying in Italy. I received this thoughtful letter signed by Monsignor L. Sandri:

Vatican City, April 7, 1995

Dear Dr. Hartmann:

I am writing at the direction of His Holiness Pope John Paul II to acknowledge the copy of your autobiography which you presented to him. I have the honor to assure you of his Holiness's gratitude for your thoughtful gesture and his appreciation for the respectful sentiments which prompted it.

About the same time, I received a book published by the Catbird Press in New Haven, Connecticut, titled *Jewish Voices, German Words: Growing Up Jewish in Postwar Germany and Austria.* The parents of the young writers in this book had survived the Holocaust and returned after the war to their native country, where the new democratic German government received them with open arms and paid them restitution. Their children grew up in postwar Germany and Austria, attending high school and going through further education there, coming to grips with their Jewish identity and fighting anti-Semitism and neo-Nazism in their country. Some of the writers are angry with their parents for returning to their native lands after being driven out and tortured by the Nazis.

Not all of the stories in *Jewish Voices, German Words* are equally impressive. One account, typical of the new Jewish generation is Katja Behrens's "Perfectly Normal." In it she talks with her German compatriots, trying to discuss the Holocaust with them. They didn't share her feelings. "'It wasn't six million,' they said, and I said, 'So what, even if it was only four,' and they said, like accountants, 'But it makes a difference,' as if only the numbers counted." She also went to her old high school teacher, although she remembered him for previous anti-Semitic remarks. When Katja brought up the subject of extermination of the Jews, he did not want to hear about it. "Let's let sleeping dogs lie," he said.

One day, Katja Behrens talked with a man her own age. He was quite a cultured church organist who had had a little bit to drink. "To get anywhere in the music world," he said, "you have to be Jewish or gay." When questioned by the author of "Perfectly Normal" if he was not wrong after so many Jews had been gassed by the Nazis, the church organist replied, "No, really, they're everywhere again, they've cornered all the key positions. What? Gassed? Not at all. They earmark all the good positions for each other. I'm telling you."

I was still thinking about *Growing Up Jewish in Postwar Germany and Austria* when I received a letter from my good friend Dr. Ronald Pies, associate clinical professor of psychiatry at Boston's Tufts University. The envelope contained the draft of his soon-to-be-published paper titled "Maimonides and the Origins of Cognitive-Behavioral Therapy." Moses Maimonides, who lived from 1135 to 1204, was born in Cordoba, Spain, which was under Muslim rule at the time. When a more fundamentalist regime came into power, the family had to flee, finally settling in Egypt. He was the greatest Jewish physician-philosopher-theologian ever, and his magnum opus is his *Guide for the Perplexed.*

In his paper about cognitive-behavioral therapy, a technique developed by Dr. Aaron Beck, Ronald Pies shows us how many of the ideas of this rational-emotive therapy were already stressed by Maimonides so many centuries before. As I wrote in my reply to the author, I enjoyed his paper very much, and I pledged to reread it from time to time.

I met Dr. Pies between ten and fifteen years ago, after he had written an article in the *Archives of General Psychiatry* about the ideas of his teacher, Professor Thomas S. Szasz. Dr. Pies was chief resident in psychiatry at the Upstate Medical Center in Syracuse, and I asked him for a reprint of his article. We have corresponded ever since. He has lectured before audiences in the United States and abroad, has published poetry, and his first psychiatric textbook bears the title *Inside Psychotherapy: The Patient's Handbook.* Not very long ago, he sent me a copy of his latest book, *Clinical Manual of Psychiatric Diagnoses and Treatment,* which I was most happy to receive. Naturally, with a busy schedule like his, Dr. Pies is not able to send me frequent letters, but whenever I receive even a short note from him, I feel enriched.

🐞 🐞 🐞

I was also quite pleased to hear recently from my good friend Dr. Otto Lippman. He is a little older than me, and he, too, received his medical training at Breslau Jewish Hospital, where I was schooled. His wife, Lilli, worked there as a nurse, as had my dear Herta. For years he was a professor of ophthalmology at the University of Austin Texas Medical College. I had sent him a copy of my review of Steven Jacobs's *Rethinking Jewish Faith: The Child of a Survivor Responds.* Dr. Lippman didn't agree with some of Jacobs's ideas, so I sent him my reply. I knew I would talk with him by telephone soon. It was Holocaust (Shoah) Memorial time, and Otto Lippman had enclosed a program for the Holocaust Remembrance Prayer Service at St. Augustine Catholic Church.

🐞 🐞 🐞

At a recent Friday night service at Temple Society of Concord, we remembered the fifty-year anniversary of the liberation of the concentration camps. At the service we honored two righteous gentiles, Henry Cumoletti and Professor Antje Lemke.

Both speakers were introduced by Rabbi Sheldon Ezring and asked questions by Marlene Holstein from those submitted by the audience. The evening was completed with Cantor Francine Berg's beautiful voice being accompanied by the guitar strings of Alison Bert, director of the guitar program at Syracuse University's School of Music.

Henry Cumoletti was born and raised in Brooklyn, New York, and moved in 1933 with his wife, Anna, to Watertown, New York. In 1946 he received a call from the U.S. War Department to become a court reporter at the Nuremberg War Trials. This assignment changed his whole life. He was unable to understand the mentality of the accused Nazi defendants, who admitted their crimes and showed no remorse. Neither could he see eye to eye with the revisionists in the United States and Canada who deny that the Holocaust ever existed. For him, as he told us, you could just as well deny the sun, the moon, the birds, and the flowers. I talked with Mr. Cumoletti after the service. Through his friend and agent Myron Liberman, I received his book of recollections titled *Crimes Against Humanity*. Mr. Cumoletti autographed the little volume for me (he also owns my autobiography). In spite of his advanced age, he continues to speak on radio, television, and before live audiences about the war trials, a topic so close to his heart.

Antje Lemke grew up in Hitler's Germany, the daughter of the well-known Protestant theologian Rudolf Bultmann. She saw how her father and the rest of the family were helping Jews by hiding them at the risk of their own lives. They also helped Jews to escape to other countries. There was no doubt in that family's mind that they had to act in accordance with their conscience and the dictates of their Christian religion. After Antje's emigration to the United States, she lectured on the evils of the Holocaust both here and across Europe. She is now professor emeritus in the School of Information Studies at Syracuse University.

Temple Society of Concord's auditorium was filled to capacity. Later, after the service, the audience met the two honored guests in the Social Hall. I had met Antje Lemke before when she gave a talk at our Soule Library. At the time, my *Once a Doctor* had not yet been published so I brought an inscribed copy with me on this occasion to give to the honored guest. As soon as she reached out her hand to take the small volume out of the bag, she remembered the full title of my autobiography. She had purchased it soon after its publication. She was very happy to accept my gift, because I had personally inscribed it for her.

The following Sunday a community Holocaust Remembrance Program was held at Temple Adath Yeshurun. There was a candle-lighting conducted by some of the survivors who had lost numerous loved ones during this dark chapter in human history. The invocation was given by Rabbi Charles Sherman, the leader of this conservative synagogue, followed by a welcome given by our County Executive Nicholas Pirro, who introduced the speaker, Joseph Kalina, a well-known local businessman whom he had known as a member of the Syracuse community for many years.

An eloquent speaker, Mr. Kalina had grown up in Slovakia, where he was arrested, imprisoned, and beaten up in concentration camps but miraculously escaped death on several occasions. He has given lectures in the United States at schools and universities and has written a book titled *Holocaust Odyssey* with Stanley R. Allen, a professor at Syracuse University. When I purchased my own copy of his work at the Jewish Community Center, I was touched by his inscription:

> To Dr. Heinz Hartmann to whom I have to say thank you for inspiring me to write this book. May you be rewarded with good health and a long life.

I just read this book in its entirety and I am so very glad I did.

Reverend Ronald Dewberry, President of the Interreligious Council and Pastor of Bethany Church, reflected on the Holocaust, while Cantor Lerner of Temple Adath Yeshurun led the large audience in the singing of the Memorial Prayer, the

"Star-Spangled Banner," and the "Hatikvah," the Hebrew Israeli song known the world over.

The musical selections were played by Alison Berg. This young lady has received a great many musical awards in the United States and abroad, but she is always prepared to perform the songs of her people when the need arises, as on this unforgettable occasion. With her was Julianna Sabol, also of Syracuse University's School of Music, whose beautiful voice sang in English, Yiddish, and Hebrew.

         🐾   🐾   🐾

People from the Christian Religious Right keep telling us that we have to forget and forgive the Holocaust, now that more than half a century has passed. Besides, we have "as real Americans" to give equal time to the Holocaust deniers or revisionists. I felt reassured about the real America when early in May of 1995 President Clinton celebrated with the Armed Forces the fiftieth anniversary of V.E. Day, to commemorate the Allied victory in Europe. For me, the high point of this anniversary celebration was the showing of the concentration camp liberation by the Allies. Here all could see for themselves the emaciated, skeletal bodies of the few survivors among the many corpses.

Then the president introduced Samuel Pisar, one of the invited guests. Pisar, now a leading international lawyer in New York and Paris, lost his father, his mother, and his little sister after the Nazis overran Soviet-occupied Poland. He himself was a survivor of several death camps, until he was finally liberated on V.E. Day by a black soldier, a descendant of slaves, who drove him and others to freedom. And at that moment Samuel Pisar called out the only few words his mother had taught him in English: "God bless America!"

Pisar worked in the 1950s for the United Nations and was an advisor for the Kennedy administration. Soon he was made a United States citizen by a special act of Congress. But it took him till about 1980—thirty-five years after liberation—to publish his memoirs of the *Shoah of Blood and Hope*. Like most survivors he was unable to make sense of his past sufferings and to write down his experiences. The pain was just too great. Understandable as it is, this lack of reporting has given revisionists a big opportunity to deny the Holocaust and to recast history in their image. We are grateful to Samuel Pisar for his memoirs.

Our good friend Judith Sternberg Newman, a former nurse at Breslau Jewish Hospital, was one of the first death camp survivors to write about her Shoah experiences. I believe I was the first person to read her diary, which she started to write soon after her liberation. I encouraged her to have her memoirs published. Her volume titled *In the Hell of Auschwitz* had its first printing by Exposition Press in 1963. In 1993 her book went into its third printing.

As discussed above, there can be no doubt in a sane person's mind that the Shoah with its destruction of six million Jews—just because they were Jews—is a horrific historical fact. Some people who call themselves friends have advised the Jews they know to "intermarry and bring up non-Jewish children." While each person must do what his or her conscience dictates, I believe a short story from my previous work will help to show the error of such a view.

In *Once a Doctor* I mentioned the story of Moses Mendelssohn, the famous German-Jewish philosopher who translated the Hebrew Scriptures into German. His grandson Felix was brought up in the Christian faith and was known all over the world for his church music. As I remember, even the descendants of this wonderful Jewish family were persecuted by the Third Reich. So the effort to change the faith of one's children won't protect them from persecution by people bent on discriminating on the basis of religious heritage.

The presence of Jews is not necessary to produce the evil of anti-Semitism. Poland, for example, was always an anti-Semitic country with its pogroms and other forms of persecution. Today, with barely a handful of Jews living within its borders, the population still blames the Jews whenever an economic crisis occurs. No, instead of hiding our Jewish identity—like all the generations before us—we are going back to our sources for strength.

These sources are, of course, the Hebrew Scriptures as well as the Mischnah and the Talmud, in addition to the sages and philosophers through the Middle Ages and into our own time. The writings of Martin Buber and Franz Rosenweig have been translated from German into English. There are also important volumes regarding our Jewish identity that were published by Abraham Joshua Heschel. Bible commentaries have been edited on the conservative side by Rabbi Joseph Hertz and, more recently, by W. Gunther Plaut, the Reformed rabbi of Toronto. Aside from these many books, which tell us what it means to be Jewish, few scholarly or popular books have been produced to help Jews understand their heritage.

One of the newer and highly recommended books is Rabbi Harold M. Schulweis's *For Those Who Can't Believe: Overcoming the Obstacles to Faith.* In this book he quotes Menachem Mendel, a rabbi of the nineteenth century: "For the believer there are no questions and for the unbeliever there are no answers." Schulweis comes to a different conclusion: "I have come to know many believers with profound doubts and many unbelievers with deep yearnings for serious answers." Among Schulweis's chapters are ones that typify the issues every Jew has had to face: "To Whom We Pray and for What," "Biblical Revelation: Did God Really Say?" and "Particularism and Universalism: Either a Jew or a Human Being." Strangely enough, I had no disagreement with the learned author concerning his religious discussions about Judaism and faith, but in reading him I came to an entirely different conclusion with respect to the importance of the best-selling physician-writer Dr. Bernie Siegel.

According to Schulweis, Siegel makes man the master of his own fate, one who can blame only himself if he does not recover. What Siegel really says to those patients who are told by their doctors that they have only a few weeks or months to live is not to believe what they are told. Many of those with dim prognoses have lived for many years after their scheduled time for departing this world. For some, their cancerous metastatic lesions subsided; for others their heart function improved. Dr. Siegel had the cases in his books to prove his point. A surgeon himself, Siegel never withheld treatment from his patients. Yet it was a long, long time until official publications of the medical establishment took notice of Siegel's books or his views. The psychiatric literature warned against *Love, Medicine, and Miracles,* claiming that some readers might get depressed and blame themselves for not having had the right attitude in overcoming their illness. Well, I for one have recommended Siegel's books, both while I was still in practice and after my retirement. Many people are grateful for his encouragement and have benefited from reading his views. I have never seen a case of depression in people who looked for help in Siegel's writings.

🐜   🐜   🐜

I have been rereading one of the most valued possessions in my Jewish book collection. It is a work titled *What Is the Purpose of Creation?: A Jewish Anthology.* The editor, Michael A. Alter, is a teacher of American history, economics, and government at Miami Southridge High School in Miami, Florida. In addition to the classical sources Alter includes in this work, he quotes from various commentators. Among them he quotes Felix Adler, Sigmund Freud, and Albert Einstein. But I think it is Abraham Joshua Heschel who Alter cites with the greatest success. This noted scholar and philosopher had earned a doctorate at the University of Berlin. After his escape from the Nazis, he taught first at the Hebrew Union College, and after 1945 he was on the faculty of the Jewish Theological Seminary of New York. He was very active in the civil rights movement and in the dialogue between Jews and Christians. Heschel wrote numerous books, but in this anthology the editor reprints an excerpt from Heschel's work titled *Man Is Not Alone.*

Why is Heschel so much more convincing than many of the other contributors? I think it is because he knew and cited all the Jewish sources. He knew the meaning of our existence as a people. As he put it, the "Bible is the record of God's approach to his people." Heschel lived Judaism, and he proved to be an example to Jews and non-Jews alike.

         ❧   ❧   ❧

Rabbi Joseph Telushkin, a prolific writer and well-known speaker, spent his long-awaited scholar-in-residence weekend in Syracuse. I listened to his first talk, which was the main lecture for the Syracuse Jewish community at Congregation Beth Scholom-Chevra Shas. Rabbi Telushkin talked in depth about his newer books and engaged in question-and-answer periods at the Jewish Orthodox Temple Beth El throughout the entire weekend. Before the start of his weekend program, he autographed copies of his books at one of our large local bookstores.

On all of these occasions, Rabbi Telushkin signed copies of his *Jewish Humor, Jewish Literacy,* and *Jewish Wisdom* books. People stood in line for a chance to speak to him. I gave him an autographed copy of my *Once a Doctor.* I figured that it would take quite a while before I would hear from him again. You can image my surprise when I received the following letter just one week later from Boulder, Colorado:

Dear Dr. Hartmann:

Thank you so much for giving me a copy of your book. It's a moving work filled with touching, insightful anecdotes, particularly of your experiences under the Nazis, and the accounts of your experiences as a physician here in America. What shines through in the book is your generosity of heart and sharpness of mind. Your family has good reason to be proud to have you as their patriarch, and I am proud to know that you are a fan of mine. Now I am a fan of yours.

With Best Wishes,
Shalom,

Joseph Telushkin

Another book that I highly recommend is *Jewish Renewal: A Path to Healing and Transformation,* written by Michael Lerner, editor of *Tikkun* magazine. The word "tikkun" means the mending of the world, which has been the task of Jews since the beginning of Jewish history. After a conservative Jewish upbringing, Lerner attended the Jewish Theological Seminary, where it was the work of Abraham Joshua Heschel that influenced him the most. Under Heschel's guidance, Lerner read G. W. F. Hegel, Martin Heidegger, Martin Buber, and many others. More importantly, Lerner read the prophets. He says of Heschel's influence: "So much of what I say in this book is a footnote and update to his thinking."

Since the beginning of time, the nations of the world were awestruck by their gods and the wonders of nature; but an unfair distribution of wealth and power along with tremendous cruelty and oppression were part of a reality with which one had to deal. The message of the Hebrew Bible (the Torah) was an entirely different one, says Lerner: "The God of the Bible is . . . based on an understanding that every single human being is infinitely precious and deserving of respect and love. Not just Jews or some special subset of humans. The Torah insists that all human beings derive from a single founding father and mother who were created in the image of the Divine."

If I have to find one fault with Lerner's book, it would be its enormous length. At nearly five hundred pages few readers will work through this volume in its entirety. If they don't, however, they will miss out on references to dozens of useful books with the same message of a Judaism based on the Hebrew Bible, searching day and night for the identity of the Jewish people. Needless to say, *Jewish Renewal* has been supported by Jewish leaders of all the various branches of Judaism, but also by non-Jewish scholars like Harvey Cox, professor of divinity at Harvard University, as well as psychiatrist, author, and lecturer M. Scott Peck, whose *The Road Less Travelled* has been on the *New York Times* best-seller list.

Some time back, I listened to two of my favorite authors,

Rabbi Marc Gellman and Monsignor Thomas Hartman, being interviewed by Charles Gibson on ABC's *Good Morning America* about their various books. *Where Does God Live?* appeared in 1991, while *How Do You Spell God?* was published in 1995. The second volume has an introduction by His Holiness the Dalai Lama, the head of Tibetan Buddhism. These two friends show us that all the religions of the world pose the same questions: How should we live? What happens after we die? Why do bad things happen to good people? How can we talk to God? and many others. It is not strange at all that the rabbi and the priest have become such close friends. But after centuries of persecuting other religions, it is ironic that the Catholic Church would be one of the first to declare that the Jewish people can find salvation in their own religion.

Needless to say, Rabbi Gellman and Monsignor Hartman approach their subject with a sense of humor. They don't believe in a religion that declares good and basically descent people to be "sinners" who are "doomed" unless they follow a particular creed. They have basically the same attitude as the Reverend Robert Schuller who, twenty-five years earlier, had been preaching "fire and brimstone" to his Protestant flock; then he heard the Reverend Norman Vincent Peale point out that there is a much better way to reach the heart of any congregation—emphasize the positive dimensions of belief. Since that time Dr. Schuller has invited Protestant guest speakers as well as Catholic and Jewish guests to address his congregation. In part, I think this is the reason so many listeners all over the world can identify with him and his message. Of course most of my Christian friends, the majority of whom try to convert me, don't consider him a Christian. He is too liberal for them.

Some people believe that religion can divide us. According to Rabbi Gellman, a religion that shows respect for others, does not look down on others who have different religious beliefs, and does not feel that it possesses the only truth is more likely to unite rather than divide us. In contrast, it is the staunchly fundamentalist Christians who do not recognize any belief except their own. They, of course, despise Jews because the "Covenant has been taken from them." In their eyes, Jews are not "real Americans" since they cannot be part of a "Christian nation." Still, they need the Jews if only in the hope of converting us. In fact, it seems that every few years various Christians are announcing the time of Armageddon, when a monumental confrontation between good and evil forces takes place and the Second Coming of Jesus as the anointed Messiah is expected to occur. If their current calculation proves to be wrong (as all the preceding ones have) and another delay of the Second Coming has to be admitted, there is always the possibility that their frustration might lead to more anti-Semitism. Without the conversion of the Jews the Second Coming cannot occur.

It was such a coincidence when I read in a summer issue of *Free Inquiry* an article by the well-known science author Martin Gardner titled "The Wandering Jew and the Second Coming." Gardner mused that "Preacher Jerry Falwell is so convinced that he will soon be raptured . . . that he once said he has no plans for a burial plot. Austin Miles, who once worked for Pat Robertson, reveals . . . that Pat once seriously considered plans to televise the Lord's appearance in the skies!" All hopes of such fundamentalist Christians are intertwined with the conversion of the Jews.

In the summer 1995 issue of the *Jewish Spectator* I found an interesting article titled "Reclaiming Missionized Jews" by Art Bernstein. A large part of the article is devoted to Jews for Jesus—what are sometimes called Messianic Jews—a group I discussed earlier. I was surprised to learn in one of his footnotes that Bernstein was once a Messianic Jew himself. Now he is "an activist for Judaism" while he lives and writes in Grants Pass, Oregon. This community is a small town to which many of my relatives on Herta's side have moved.

16

There Is Health and Then There Is Well-Being

Reflecting on the topic of medicine, I feel the need to discuss my son, Michael's, special situation, since he is not able to speak for himself.

Michael continues to be a patient at the Jewish Home of Central New York, which is just a short distance from our home. The facility is under the able directorship of Mr. Harvey Finkelstein who, with his expert guidance, supervises the medical staff. One can depend on the excellent and heartwarming care of the dedicated nurses who work at the facility. Not long ago, in an effort to better serve the needs of a growing patient group, the home opened its new Alzheimer Unit offering individualized care and attention to each person afflicted with this devastating disease.

Although we have all the confidence in the world in Michael's treatment at the Jewish Home, our good friend Eleene Seeber remains always at his side, cooperating with the nursing staff on a daily basis.

As soon as Michael developed severe symptoms—so severe in fact that he required hospitalization—I decided to apply for admission to the home. Since Michael moved to these new surroundings, he has remained on a regimen of Dilantin combined with Phenobarbital to control his seizures. Periodic blood tests determine if the dose of anticonvulsant needs to be increased or decreased. Fortunately, his seizures remain well under control.

In fair weather Eleene or one of the nurses will take Michael for a ride in his wheelchair on the spacious grounds of the facility so he can be out in the sunshine and enjoy some fresh air. Michael amuses himself by watching his favorite programs on television, and he often enjoys the daily entertainment and activity programs that the Jewish Home provides. On Friday nights, as well as on Sabbath and on high holidays, he can be taken to the synagogue services. The home also provides religious services appropriate for Protestant and Catholic residents.

If Michael happens to need something in a hurry, there is a little store in the building to meet the basic needs of both patients and visitors. The men have a barber available to them whenever they might need a haircut.

Family members and friends take turns visiting with Michael at the Jewish Home. They provide a frequent diversion and stimulation for him. So, even though his limitations are considerable, Michael continues to enjoy a happy life.

๑   ๑   ๑

While Michael takes just a few medications to stabilize his condition, I continue to take a large variety of drugs under the careful supervision of Drs. Gould and Kronenberg. After being placed on the coronary reversal therapy, it took a while for me to get used to the regimented diet, but now I enjoy my low-fat meals. I am permitted ten to fifteen grams of fat per day combined with at least sixty grams of protein from nonfat dairy products and low levels of carbohydrates. The cholesterol in my blood is meticulously regulated with the help of the semi-vegetarian diet and the dosage of Zocor. A bit of fish and the occasional turkey are permitted, but for quite a while now I have not cared to eat fish or fowl at all. Remaining lean is a requirement, as is exercise. I still take the antihypertensive drugs Norvasc and Vasotec as well as an anti-angina medication, but all are ingested in moderate doses. I continue taking Dyazide to prevent water retention. Smoking is, of course, prohibited, but since I never used tobacco it hasn't been a problem for me.

Like many people with heart and coronary problems, I take aspirin therapy. While this has become a constant in my daily routine, I have yet to become accustomed to the required amounts of vitamins I must consume. Aside from one multivitamin per day, I must take 30 mg of beta carotene, 800 mg of vitamin E, and 1000 mg of vitamin C. These supplements provide nutrients that my restrictive diet cannot replenish in adequate amounts. Each month the laboratory tests continue to be performed to determine my level of the bad cholesterol (LDL) and the good cholesterol (HDL), as well as tests for triglycerides and liver function.

No doubt some readers might find mine to be a tedious existence, but this is my life now, and I have to go on.

My total cholesterol level on the coronary reversal program should be less than 140 mg, which is much lower than internists or cardiologists suggest. But it is carefully monitored to maintain a level of cholesterol that assists the reversal therapy, thus preventing the need for invasive surgery.

While my medications seem to have been stabilized and my diet is under control, I have experienced more frequent angina attacks in recent years. The terrible summer heat and humidity we often endure here in upstate New York is the culprit. To control for this, and to maintain my comfort, we often have to set the thermostat to a much lower setting than the average person would prefer. Of course, there are always unforeseen situations arising—the occasional power outage will find us scurrying to call a local repair service to restore our climate control to normal.

In the autumn the number of angina attacks I experience dramatically reduces. In the hope of achieving better control

of the climate in the house, we purchased a small ther-
mometer-hygrometer, which shows us at a glance the inside
and outside temperatures as well as the humidity level indoors.
Joan also sought the advice of weather experts at the local television stations regarding the heat setting for the thermostat
during the night or how to set the air conditioner when the
temperature would rise during the day.

No matter how careful one is with medications, the periodic tests will show fluctuations in their various levels, thus
requiring that the dosage of one drug be reduced while that of
another might need to be slightly increased. Once, when my
vasodilator drug was reduced and my hypertension and pulse-
slowing medication was increased, the change caused my
pulse to drop to forty-five beats per minute, while at other
times it was irregular. With assurances from my doctors and a
bit of tweaking, my pulse rate stabilized.

Once, when I had a chest cold, I made the mistake of
taking an over-the-counter medication, which caused considerable discomfort. When Dr. Gould was called, he explained,
in his usual soothing way, that the medicine I took was a vaso-
constrictor that countered the effect of the medications he and
Dr. Kronenberg had prescribed for me. I had to discontinue the
cold medication immediately. A word of warning to those on
prescription medications: make sure you consult your physician before taking over-the-counter remedies. It could save
you a lot of trouble later, as I found out the hard way.

During a heatwave one June, the Isordil (40 mg four times
daily) didn't seem to help. Dr. Gould, in cooperation with Dr.
Kronenberg, changed the medication to Imdur (60 mg twice
daily) and I was advised to take my Nitrostat if a stressful situation arose. Admittedly, it isn't easy to keep track of all these
medications. But I am not alone. Joan sees to my special diet
and my regime of medications. When the grandchildren were
here they would assist with checking my blood pressure and
pulse. With so many people to help, I never had to worry about
running out of vital medications. I hope that elders living alone
have a good support system of family and friends who can

help them keep up with their medication schedules. Even with the best of intentions, one forgets to take a pill now and again, but a good support system can make all the difference.

♠   ♠   ♠

Sometimes my local friends find it hard to reach me because Joan is on the telephone to Dr. Gould each week while he patiently answers all of our questions. Some of my frequent local callers are former patients. Others are immigrants from Nazi Germany whom I have known for decades: Rita Seligmann, daughter Esther, and grandson Kenny; Heinz Rothschild; our old neighbor Louis De Stefano and his daughter Louise; our devoted friend Shirley Small and her daughter Barbara; our friend Dr. Marsha Snyder, whom we know from Temple Society of Concord and through her medical work; and, last but not least, our good friend Roz Sagar, whom we met with her late husband, Ian, decades ago at the Association for Retarded Children and at Temple Society of Concord. Michael, one of Ms. Sagar's sons, suffers from Downs Syndrome and is a good friend of our Michael. These good friends, and many more I have no doubt failed to mention, have helped make my life tremendously fulfilling even when it seems that each day brings new struggles and physical challenges.

Our friend Paul Bloomfield, whom we met originally at Temple Society of Concord, has retired from his contracting job and moved to California. But never a week goes by that he doesn't telephone us to inquire about our well-being. Mrs. Lorraine Sher, now retired as director of religious education at Temple Concord, would refer me to high school and college students who wanted to know more about the Holocaust. She always goes out of her way to send me audio-and videotapes of special occasions so that I can stay in touch with the congregation.

I was especially pleased to have a visit not long ago from our temple Cantor, Francine Berg. Not only did she bring along audiocassettes of Jewish folk music and an album of sheet music for Sarah, but she had two tapes of Friday night services for me. On one dated July 19, 1995, she was the featured soloist who also accompanied the Temple Concord Shalom Singers. The tape was dedicated to me. Rabbi Ezring wanted to honor me because of my illness. He prayed at the end of the service for my complete recovery. I feel privileged that he and the congregation should bestow such an honor on me.

Temple Concord is a Reformed congregation in which everyone has his or her own ideas about the effect of prayer. It is hard to believe that God would change the course of any illness due to someone's prayer. But I fervently believe that the patient's attitude will be strengthened and his response to medication improved with the knowledge that friends and loved ones care deeply and are praying for him.

On the second tape Ms. Berg recorded, Rabbi Ezring was not present; he was on a planned trip to Israel with some members of the congregation. Even though his responsibilities are many and his burdens considerable, Rabbi Ezring never forgets to lend a hand to members of his congregation and to others, whenever help or empathy is needed. I can never forget how often he visited and communicated with Michael, both during my son's long hospital stay and at the Jewish home.

I and my family are indeed fortunate to be visited by people like Bobbi Smiley Lutz, who graduated with Joan from Syracuse Central High School over thirty years ago. She came from Simi Valley, California, where she resides with her husband, Helmut, and their grown children. Bobbi flew in alone for a few days to be with her two aunts, the only surviving sisters of her late mother. Though she was only to be in town for a very short time, Bobbi made sure to come see us the day before she had to depart for home. She had not seen Joan for a few years, and she know that I was not well. We all felt enriched by Bobbi's delightful visit.

And on one of Sarah's birthdays her friend Michele, who went to college with her in Syracuse quite a few years ago, dropped by for a visit. Michele had continued her studies in Arizona and enlisted in the Air Force, where she met Todd Putnam, who also came to see us that day. They are both stationed in South Carolina, but planned a reaffirmation of their wedding vows at a local Methodist church the following Saturday. Sarah was quite excited to be one of the bride's maids.

Across the table from Michele and Todd sat another birthday guest, a young lady quite illustrious in her own way. Deanna, who is legally blind, graduated with high honors in Sarah's class at Le Moyne College. She planned to pursue postgraduate studies at Syracuse University in the hope of making a career for herself as a counselor, helping others. Next to Deanne, as always, was Page, her seeing-eye dog. What a dedicated companion.

Deanna is always in a good mood. She never seems to complain about anything. She does her homework with the help of people who read to her, and she is assisted by her computer, which translates the written word into Braille for her. Sarah sometimes attends movies or "sees" a home movie with Deanna. They went to a nearby restaurant for Sarah's birthday dinner. Sarah, Maurice, and Deanna went without Joan or me, since I still must keep to my prescribed diet—meals that can only be prepared at home. They were joined later by Sarah's friend David LaRocco and his parents, who had driven from Virginia to move him into a new apartment near Syracuse University's Newhouse School of Communications. The next day, after the moving was completed, David, his parents, and his fourteen-year-old sister (also named Sarah) visited with us.

🪲   🪲   🪲

It was such a pleasure to find in one of our local papers a fine article about one of our friends Dr. Fredrick Roberts, who was Joan's pediatrician and later took care of Sarah and Maurice when they were growing up. Now at age seventy-six he planned to open an office where he would work singlehandedly caring for underprivileged children. His younger colleagues would take over his active practice.

Dr. Roberts has five children and six grandchildren, and his wife wholeheartedly supports this dream of his. As long as he can meet his office expenses, he would be satisfied. Dr. Roberts planned to see patients between the ages of five and seventeen so that he won't have the many emergency calls so common with youngsters under age five. As reporter Amber Smith so ably described, the doctor would concentrate on "learning disabilities, speech and language development, hearing loss, drug and alcohol problems, and psychiatric disorders." With the Jewish New Year approaching, I sent our best wishes to him and his family, and for the success of his endeavor. Dr. Roberts soon phoned me to describe his plans in more detail. He hoped to find suitable and reasonable office space in the near future. He looked forward to possibly publishing his memoirs as a pediatrician.

I also received two special Rosh Hashana surprises: One was a call from our good friend Judith Sternberg Newman, who resides in Rhode Island. She was a chief nurse at the Breslau Jewish Hospital pediatric ward and the author of the noted memoir *In the Hell of Auschwitz*. The other surprise was an unexpected chapter of my friend Dr. Eric Kohler's manuscript about Jewish physicians caught in Germany during the Third Reich. Dr. Kohler hoped to have a volume published within a reasonable time. I had mentioned his intended publication in my autobiography, but so far his duties as acting chair and professor of history at the University of Wyoming have prevented him from finishing the manuscript.

In the chapter Dr. Kohler sent me he reported on the majority of Jewish physicians. The ones who were in private practice were in hospital positions or teaching in leading universities. I belonged to the much smaller group of medical students waiting (unsuccessfully) for a medical license and to graduate from medical school. Luckily, I was permitted to graduate from the University of Berne, Switzerland, and then to emigrate to the United States and to become licensed as a physician in America.

Although I was not able to compare the life of a practicing physician in Germany with one in private practice in America, I was able to introduce Dr. Kohler to many of the older physicians, whom he later contacted while conducting research for his manuscript. There was Dr. Julius Krombach, who practiced in Syracuse for many years until he retired to Florida, where he later died at the age of ninety-four. Dr. Kohler also communicated with Dr. Rudolf Stern, a former professor of medicine at Breslau Medical College. Later Dr. Kohler was to find out much about the medical history of my long-lost cousin, the well-known forensic pathologist Dr. Werner Spitz of Detroit, when he telephoned the doctor's mother, Dr. Anna Spitz, now well into her nineties. Naturally, I look forward to future chapters that Dr. Kohler will send me, and eventually the entire completed manuscript.

17

Of Beliefs and Actions

One of two books I recently read is a small paperback that appeared in its second edition under the title *Darwin on Trial.* It is written by Phillip E. Johnson, a professor of law at University of California at Berkeley. He was a featured speaker at a service held in Reverend Robert Schuller's Crystal Cathedral. Johnson bemoans the teaching of evolution in our schools as fact and that scientists like Carl Sagan and others "misuse Darwin's theory of evolution to promote atheism." On the other hand, "a great many religious leaders accept evolution on scientific grounds without relinquishing their belief in religious principles." While I doubt that learned scientists seek to convert young minds to atheism through the vehicle of Darwin's theory of evolution, there is abundant anecdotal evidence from those in the fields of religion and science that one's religious beliefs can be held simultaneously with acceptance of scientifically supported views on how humans and other species evolved.

And this is, of course, as it should be. In accordance with Jewish tradition, there has never been a clash between Judaism and science, except for those few ultra-Orthodox Jews for whom the Bible stands or falls with the belief in a God who created the world in exactly six days and then rested on the Sabbath. The Darwinian theory focuses on broad issues of species evolution and diversification; it can not and does not attempt to explain how a flower grows or the extraordinary development of the human heart and brain. Nor can any scientific theory explain our inner voice—the conscience that helps direct our actions. Recently, I had occasion to read in the multivolume nineteenth-century *Jewish Encyclopedia* and the various volumes of the twentieth-century *Encyclopedia Judaica* various articles about evolution, and all of my convictions were basically confirmed. One rabbi of the Talmud even quoted the Kabbalah, a mystical book, coming to the conclusion that God had built and destroyed other worlds ages ago, before He or She created this one. Some secrets of our world we shall never be able to disclose, and I am satisfied with that, not being a scientist myself.

The second book that I wish to discuss here has been edited by the well-known rabbi and author Jack Riemer under the title *Wrestling with the Angel: Jewish Insights on Death and Mourning.* What does the Jewish tradition tell us, the living, about comforting those who grieve, and what does it say about an afterlife? Rabbi Riemer's book is a continuation of his previous work titled *Reflection on Death,* and it brings us the stories of contemporary well-known Jewish authors who have encountered near-death situations.

One of the remarkable stories in *Jewish Insights on Death and Mourning* is told by Rabbi Harold Schulweis. He calls his chapter "Coronary Connections." After suffering a severe heart attack, Schulweis found himself in the hospital "surrounded by catheters, monitors, and needles." He was faced with the real possibility of complete disability and death. He remembered the old traditional Jewish prayers and, out of his initial fear, he turned to them and gained understanding. Schulweis was thinking about the wonders of the heart and was no longer afraid. He learned more from his illness than from many of the books he read, although the books laid the foundation for his confrontation with death and ultimately his ardent desire to live. In Judaism life is holy. As the Talmud declared centuries ago, it is even permissible to desecrate the Sabbath in order to save a life. Schulweis also learned from his experience that friendship, both in our own families and in the general community, is "sacred." A letter, a card, a prayer, a call, or a visit can be "as therapeutic as the cleverest of medicines."

Another interesting chapter of Rabbi Riemer's book is written by famed author and rabbi Lawrence Kushner. His "A Wake-Up Call" describes a man who, because of some severe eye symptoms, was examined by an ophthalmic neurologist and subsequently diagnosed with an optic nerve lesion. He was told by his physicians that this lesion could be the forerunner of a brain tumor. Although the follow-up test came back negative and his disease was dubbed "idiopathic," since its cause could not be determined, the man treasured life even more, since he had narrowly escaped the possibility of death. He knew that anybody could die at any given moment. "You are alive right now. Beyond that, there simply are no guarantees." According to Kushner, "Only the certainty of our death and the possibility that it can come at any time make life precious." He also mentions a Rabbi Simha Bunim who, as he lay dying, took his wife's hand and said, "Why are you crying? My whole life was only that I might learn how to die."

In a beautiful short story titled "Should We Tell the Patient the Truth?" well-known psychiatrist Samuel Klagbrun tells the readers of Rabbi Riemer's book about an elderly German-born Jewish couple who had been married for fifty years, and throughout their many years together they always spoke the truth to each other. As it happened, the woman was dying from metastatic cancer, and her husband found a noted physician who would accept his wife for treatment but with one condition: the doctor would discontinue the woman's treatment if ever the husband were to tell her the truth about her prognosis. "It is cruel to tell a patient," the doctor believed.

Yet the wife realized how her health was failing and felt that her husband was hiding something from her. Finally, in a state of delirium, she accused her husband of being a traitor to their long-held promise not to have secrets. She eventually died in a paranoid state, and her husband suffered a major depression. He came for treatment to Dr. Klagsbrun, who made him see the terrible injustice the doctor had done to both him and his wife. No one should have to give up the promise of a lifetime in exchange for treatment.

A story of touching brotherly love is told by Marshall Meyer in "Let Them Know What You Want." Rabbi Meyer was a leader of Latin-American Jewry, who had travelled from Argentina to donate a kidney to his brother, John, who was dying with cancer. Unfortunately, he arrived too late to help save his brother; the cancer had already spread to John's liver. The rabbi stayed with his brother for another month to nurse him while John continued receiving chemotherapy and radiation at Yale University Hospital in New Haven, Connecticut. As John's condition deteriorated, Marshall Meyer took his brother for radiation treatments every day, although it took him over an hour each time to get John dressed and to position him in the car for the trip. Marshall asked the doctor—a friend of both men since their childhood—why it was necessary to take a dying man for radiation treatment every day. "Because I can't stand not to do anything," was the reply. But his physician/friend advised Marshall to ask his brother what he wanted. John knew that he was dying: "Just leave me in my bed. You know what I want. I just want some music, I just want to rest." John died three weeks later at the age of forty-nine. He died "listening to all his favorite arias and all his favorite operas, and he went into a coma. And that's what he wanted." Rabbi Meyer would have felt overwhelming guilt if he had continued treatments against his brother's wishes.

This hard experience with his brother made Rabbi Meyer realize how important it is for people to have living wills. "You owe it to the people you love to say it in writing if you don't want heroic methods, or if you do want to fight for life until the last breath, if you are willing to stay paralyzed without speech or brain dead for six years. . . . You owe it to those you love to let them know." Rabbi Meyer, whose exemplary life was always devoted to others, died in New York in 1994.

I didn't know that soon after discussing *Jewish Insights on Death and Mourning* some of the concerns addressed in that powerful book would become quite personal when the news flashed that Israel's Prime Minister Yizhak Rabin had been assassinated. A young Jewish law student had committed the crime, fulfilling what he claimed to be a "commandment of God." Having been the man who had won the Six Day War against the extraordinary forces of neighboring Arab nations, at the time of his death Rabin was convinced that only a just peace between all the nations of the Middle East would lead to a happy coexistence.

The huge funeral, attended by throngs of people, made everyone see just how great this man was. Who could forget the beautiful words of President Clinton, who used the Hebrew term *chaver* to describe his friend. Clinton invited all the former U.S. presidents to accompany him to the funeral. There were representatives from all nations of the world who strive for peace. It was extremely moving to listen to all the eulogies, and heart-wrenching to see the agonized faces of Rabin's widow, Leah, and his daughter and son. But no eye was dry when the late prime minister's seventeen-year-old granddaughter gave her eloquent farewell. I am confident that Rabin's successor, Shamon Perez, continued to work for peace until national elections put Benjamin Netanyahu in the prime minister's office.

🐜   🐜   🐜

I remember being unable to write for one entire day because I was watching the "Million Man March on Washington," originally planned and initiated by Muslim minister Louis Farakhan. Many whites and blacks did not anticipate a very peaceful march, given Farakhan's history of making anti-Semitic remarks. Just consider what he said on a radio broadcast over a decade ago in 1984: "The Jews don't like Farakhan, so they call him Hitler. Well, that's a good name. Hitler was a very great man." In June of the same year, he remarked at the National Press Club that "Judaism is a dirty religion," and in recent years, he spoke of the Jewish people as "blooksuckers." It is no wonder, then, that the Anti-Defamation League and other Jewish organizations consider him anti-Semitic.

On the other hand, Farakhan's answers were very cordial when he was interviewed on the *Larry King Show* not all that long ago. And at the end of the "Million Man March," Minister Farakhan declared in a speech of more than two and a half hours that Christianity and Islam were very much indebted to Judaism, Father Abraham, Moses, and the Ten Commandments since they laid the foundation for the teachings of both daughter-religions. He also told the crowd that he had made a remark that he regretted, but it had come out of his mouth and he could not take it back anymore. I sincerely believe that this has happened with his previous anti-Semitic utterances. We all can learn from this unfortunate example. We must guard our tongues before speaking about other people.

Actually, the size of the crowd at the march on Washington impressed many, even though it did not reach the million mark. The participants were decent people, walking arm in arm together, not blaming others but looking inside themselves, admonishing themselves to support and not abandon their families, and not to resort to violence. They also warned against the abuse of drugs and alcohol.

      🐾   🐾   🐾

In the United States the highly conservative segment of the Republican party used as their spokesperson the news-commentator-turned-presidential-candidate Patrick Buchanan, the darling of the Religious Right.

I have in front of me the *Jewish Observer* of February 29, 1996, a part of the *New York Times* of March 3, 1996, and the March 1 edition of *Aufbau*. This is what Ms. Mollie Leitzes, editor of the *Jewish Observer,* wrote in her editorial:

The fact that [Patrick Buchanan] is most likely not electable
in no way makes his rhetoric, his tone, his nasty alluding to
"New York Bankers" (read that "Jews") any less damaging.
. . . He has spoken against loan guarantees for Israel. He has
said that the demands for greater sensitivity to Jewish issues
"is becoming a joke." . . . It is easy to dismiss Buchanan,
taking comfort in the fact that he is not likely to be elected.
But the political climate in which this kind of demagogue
finds sustenance is not altogether a safe place for Jews. . . .

How wrong the Christian Right is! But, while Pat Robertson
likes the Jews somehow in order to convert them later, Patrick
Buchanan is definitely an anti-Semite. In one of the papers I
kept on file in my library is the statement by Buchanan that the
existence of extermination camps was a technical impossi-
bility, and that equal time should be given to the former S.S.
to stress their point of the story. Most readers and students of
world history will remember how General Eisenhower felt
when he liberated the concentration camps and saw the emaciated bodies of the prisoners. There was no doubt in his mind
who the victims were, and who the killers were.

How can anyone call themselves a Christian who does not
seem to realize that both Christianity and Islam are derived
from Judaism, and that Jesus and his disciples quoted the Torah
on many occasions. But just as important is another question,
discussed in Ms. Leitzes's editorial: How is it possible that so
many people gave their vote to a notorious anti-Semite running
for the office of president of the United States? Did they ever
consider the fate of the Jews when casting their vote?

The *Sunday Times* article of March 3, 1996, discusses the
views of the Roman Catholic Church on Patrick Buchanan.
"The Catholic Church hierarchy is happy about Buchanan's
opposition to abortion, but little else. For now, criticism is
muted." The article mentioned that TV news personality Ted
Koppel, on a recent report on *Nightline* mentioned that
Buchanan's father had been "a regular listener to the anti-
Semitic broadcasts of Father Coughlin." Bay Buchanan, the

candidate's sister and manager of his presidential campaign, assailed the ABC report on her brother as "lies," calling Koppel an "anti-Catholic bigot" and denying that her father listened to the Coughlin broadcasts. Mr. Koppel said her charges were "hysterical" as well as "repugnant, unfair, and absolutely untrue."

I have listened to Ted Koppel's *Nightline* for many years. I never heard him asking unfair or insulting questions of any guest. The level of trust that the public invests in him is so high that *Nightline* became a must program to watch during the Iran hostage crisis, when the poor relatives of the hostages and the American people at large were eager to keep up with any news that he was able to impart.

I searched my memory and all the papers I saved over the years and finally found some biographical material on Ted Koppel. He was born to German parents who escaped Hitler's tyranny. They later emigrated to the United States. Koppel received his bachelors degree in journalism from Syracuse University and took postgraduate studies at Stanford University, where he received his master's degree. At Stanford he also met a Roman Catholic girl and later married her. They have four grown children. At a pivotal time in his career he took a lengthy period of time off from his anchor job to relieve his wife from her household duties so that she would be able to finish law school. Is this an "anti-Catholic bigot"?

I have in front of me the *Aufbau* article of March 1, 1996. Here, Bud Hockenberg, a Jewish activist in Des Moines, Iowa, states:

> Pat Buchanan has a very strong hate message and [a] message of class warfare. . . . Pat Buchanan poses a great danger for the Jewish community. . . . [He] has shunned the Jewish community during his campaign. The . . . presidential aspirant was the only declared Republican candidate to decline an invitation to speak to a National Jewish coalition forum last year. . . .
>
> Buchanan has riled the Jewish community for his

defense of accused Nazi war criminals. He has questioned
the number of Jews gassed at Treblinka. . . . Kenneth Stern
of the American Jewish Committee, writing in a 1991
report, described him as a man who is "no friend of the Jews
and has serious problems with Jewish issues. . . . Pat
Buchanan is one of the most dangerous anti-Semites in
America today. . . . The anti-Semitic models on which he
has based his conservatism combine to produce a man with
a severe Jewish problem. . . ."

I remember so well the story of one of the Jewish sages
who told his students to mend their ways one day before they
die. "How do we know which day we die?" a student asked.
"That's just it," said the sage, "so start mending your ways
today!"

      🐛   🐛   🐛

In an odd twist of circumstances, I was grateful during this
time to receive a "thank you" note from Rabbi Daniel Syme,
author of *Finding God.* He had been one of the scholars-in-res-
idence at Temple Society Concord and, as is my practice, I
gave him an autographed copy of my *Once a Doctor* at the
time of his lectures. Rabbi Syme's lecture series was titled "A
Conversation with God." Later he spoke on "What Happens
After I Die?" and he made a point of discussing suicide prevention with interested teenagers. In his note of November 5,
1995, he wrote:

> Thank you for your thoughtful gift of self, conveyed
> through the memories of a lifetime of caring. . . . I consider
> myself fortunate to have met you and shall cherish your
> book as a story that must be told.

      🐛   🐛   🐛

Winter was upon us—the start of the cold season. Ironically,
this is a time when I experience fewer angina attacks. But even

with this small reprieve from the humidity of summer, winter can bring some nights when I suffer chest discomfort. Joan monitors the local weather experts to ascertain the dewpoint: inevitably my discomfort relates to heightened humidity levels even in winter. We are now better able to keep up with changes in climatic conditions since a dear friend of many years generously provided us with a fax machine to help with obtaining information relevant to my health. We appreciate his thoughtful gift and will treasure it.

𝕒   𝕒   𝕒

Like anyone who is confined with an illness, my spirits rise when I receive good letters. Just such a letter came from Danyel Thomson, one of the students who led a class at Solvay High School, where I talked to sophomores about my book and the Nazi atrocities. I think she liked to learn about the essential differences between Judaism and the evangelical Christian tradition in which she was raised. She mentioned in her letter how very upset she was at the loss of her dog, Wagner, which was fatally hit by a car. I assured her that we, too, had experienced a similar loss and in much the same way.

We have a fifteen-year-old cat and a nine-year-old Dachshund named Fritzi. Both of them spend much of their day in the house. The family wanted me to have a personal pet that was younger—one with which I could build a personal rapport. No doubt they read that pets are helpful to heart patients in lowering blood pressure and aiding in relaxation.

Sarah went to the local animal shelter and returned with a rather large Labrador Retriever-type. It was both friendly and very lively. Sarah had felt sorry for it because most patrons of such shelters want puppies. Sarah was sure that Lady (or Hava, as we called her) felt left out. We only had Hava for a brief two weeks when I noticed that she was running from room to room. What she really needed was a house with a big yard so she could run and play. Reluctantly, we returned her to the shelter. Fortunately, she was soon in the hands of eager owners with all the space she needed. About a week later Sarah brought home a nine-week-old male Cocker Spaniel. Isaac has been a good friend to me and a delight to the whole family.

18

Maintaining Contact

There is always correspondence to be answered between Hanukkah and the New Year, whether it be from former patients, family, or friends both new and old. Some barely keep in touch once a year, but everyone who takes the time to remember me any time during the year deserves an immediate reply. I try as hard as I can not to disappoint anyone.

Many of our friends and relatives who communicate with us on a regular basis use the holiday season and the new year to express their feelings of love and warm friendship. I try to reciprocate by letter as my health and circumstances permit. Ilse Lewin, a distant relative and a close friend from California, had not written us for quite some time—which was a source of some concern—but we learned, upon receiving her letter, that she had apparently recovered from various ailments, which was certainly a pleasure to know. And just as we had it in mind to send our best holiday wishes to Bobbi Lutz and family, a new year's letter arrived from her. It was a wonderful surprise and we were happy to respond. I kept in regular touch with my friend Eric Kohler to see how his manuscript was coming along; and Dr. Ron Pies sent his best from Tufts

University. Not only has Dr. Pies published works in his field of psychiatry, but he is an accomplished poet and has just completed a novel about his research subject Maimonides.

Such festive seasons are the times to catch up on the lives of good friends such as ophthalmologist Dr. Otto Lippmann and wife, Lilli. Their son (a psychiatrist) and daughter (a neurologist) live out of state. During a telephone conversation, Otto and Lilli mentioned that they had received a 1995 edition of a newspaper founded decades ago in Tel Aviv by Jews who had lived and were persecuted by the Nazis in Breslau. This particular edition contained articles by Dr. Siegmund Hadda, a well-known surgeon who found a way to get out of the Theresienstadt camp and fled to freedom in the United States. There were also interesting articles about our Jewish Hospital in Breslau as well as descriptions of the last Jews, whose relatives had been unable to emigrate and were caught by the Gestapo.

Otto and Lilli were surprised to learn that I had the same issue of the Tel Aviv paper. I had subscribed to the biweekly *Aufbau,* dealing with the whereabouts and the lives of former German Jews. This special edition had been sent to me by Erwin Zadik and his wife, Ursula. Erwin had been my former classmate from the Breslau elementary school. He and his wife lived in the Bronx. Before they visited me on my seventieth birthday, we had lost contact with each other for more than sixty years.

I mentioned to the Lippmanns the title of Breslau native Judith Sternberg Newman's book *In the Hell of Auschwitz* and her status as a former nurse at the Breslau Jewish Hospital. To my astonishment, neither Otto nor Lilli had ever heard of Judith's book, nor were they sure that they remembered her from the German hospital. Naturally, I called Judy in Rhode Island right away to ask if she could send the Lippmanns a copy of her book. I also gave the Lippmanns her address so they could get in touch.

Holiday wishes continued to come in from Grazyna Widman and her family in Albany, New York. Grazyna had graduated from Syracuse University nearly thirty years ago.

Both she and Joan had majored in special education.

One of the highlights of recent holiday memory was in 1996 when Danyel Thomson and Briana Wentworth paid us a visit. When they were still in high school, I had spoken to their sophomore class on topics related to my book *Once a Doctor.* Danyel was attending Wesleyan College in North Carolina and planned to pursue a law degree, while Briana was taking premed courses in Albany. I kept in touch with Briana from time to time, I was in contact with Danyel a bit more often due to our mutual curiosity with each other's religious traditions (Danyel is an evangelical Christian). Both ladies had a profound interest in the Holocaust and had studied the works of Eli Weisel and Victor Frankl. Danyel had taken classes in comparative religion.

Danyel and Briana spent the week between Christmas and New Year's in Syracuse, where they have relatives. It was wonderful that they chose to spend a Sunday afternoon with us to catch up on each other's lives. Both young ladies had met Joan and Sarah when my daughter and granddaughter accompanied me to Solvay High School to speak with Danyel and Briana's classmates.

To add to the festive mood of the season, we received greetings from our cousins Dr. and Mrs. Werner Spitz of Detroit, Michigan. You will recall that Dr. Spitz is a forensic pathologist who is often called upon to consult throughout the United States and Canada on specific cases, and he lectures in Europe, Japan, Israel, and other countries.

19

Judaism and the Bible

I would like to begin by discussing the work by David J. Wolpe titled *Why Be Jewish?* The Bible portrays the origin of Judaism in God's call to Abraham, who is "told to leave his childhood home, told to go to the land that I will show you. The life that he has known is overthrown in this instant. Abraham has been fated to follow something grander and deeper." Judaism's most important teaching is that each human being is created in the image of God. This was a revolutionary statement even far into the Middle Ages, among the other nations, where murderers were punished in accordance with the victim's social status (those in the aristocracy were considered more worthy than mere peasants).

The Bible or Torah, on the other hand, insists that "the intrinsic value of each individual life is the same. The first demand made of a Jew is goodness. Wolpe reminds us that the Book of Leviticus states that we have an obligation to others: "You shall not pick your vineyard bare; you shall leave (the fallen fruit) to the stranger." This philosophy of goodness was unique to Judaism. Before the Sinai revelation, the people of the other nations assumed that their gods only cared about sacrifice and prayer.

No less than thirty-six times the Torah admonishes us to be kind toward strangers, reminding the Israelites that they were strangers in the land of Egypt. "You shall be Holy for I the Lord your God am holy . . . do not deal falsely with one another" (Lev. 19:1,11). Wolpe reminds us that "being smart or creative or profound will not make one good. Devotees of literature and music and art have done terrible things to their fellow human beings in this world: the murderous commandants of Auschwitz went home and listened to Bach and Mozart. Philosophy alone will not produce goodness. . . ."

One of the main messages we get from Wolpe's book is this: "The Jewish people came out of Egypt bearing a message and a mission. The message was the highest truth—of one God, a God who cares for human beings and who is passionately concerned about what to do. The mission was to bring the world to recognize that highest truth. . . .Today the Jewish mission is not diminished. In a world that still cries out for healing, where narrowness and suffering are endemic, to be chosen means to have a special calling to teach that all human beings are children of God created in God's image and must be treated as sacred. . . no nation, great or small, has touched humanity more deeply than the tiny nation of Isaiah and Jeremiah. . . ."

Chosenness in the Jewish tradition, according to Rabbi Wolpe, is not a privilege to boast about but a holy task to be undertaken. The Jewish people have to keep constantly in mind the words of the prophet Micah who said, "God has declared, O Man, what is good and what the Lord requires of you—to do justice, to love mercy, and to walk humbly with your God." How timely this discussion is, since I write this on the first day of Passover, which commemorates the Exodus of the Jews from Egypt after our liberation from slavery.

Rabbi Wolpe reminds us that until the collapse of the Soviet Union, Jews who traveled there tried to smuggle in copies of the Torah in old clothes or hidden in secret luggage compartments. This ancient old Hebrew text was banned in the Soviet Union. This powerful nation feared the sacred word of the Hebrew Bible, whose teachings profoundly changed the world and continues everyday to change the lives of people everywhere.

Wolpe reminds us that the Holocaust, in which one-third of all the world's Jews were killed, started in "one of the most progressive societies in the world at that time—Germany. It was not only another proof of the virulence of anti-Semitism, but its own progress and enlightenment. . . . We remember the haters not only for what they did but for what they could not do; they could not crush the vitality of the Jewish spirit or destroy the religious vigor of the Jewish people. . . ."

Jewish thinkers such as the German-Jewish scholar Leo Baeck called Judaism a religion of "ethical optimism." In spite of all the suffering in the world, Jews still hope that this world will be "far better than it is today." And Jewish prophets have given us the concept of a messiah. Throughout the ages, some Jews have believed in a personal messiah, while others have predicted a messianic age. In the meantime, it is up to all of us to work hard and to be worthy of such a time. While Judaism believes in the afterlife, we cannot truly know what awaits us. No matter what one believes, it is ethical action that counts. All righteous people have a share in the world to come.

"Why should one be Jewish?" Rabbi Wolpe asks in his conclusion. "Judaism . . . can teach us spiritual and moral mindfulness . . . and also encourages ethical action. But finally, the answer to why be Jewish must reside in the mystery of each seeking soul trying to find its place with others and with God." Rabbi Wolpe's slim volume (barely ninety-seven pages, with a bibliography) reminds us that a book need not be long to be enriching.

The reader should realize now that a person born into Judaism can only find fulfillment in the Jewish faith. The late astronomer Carl Sagan believed that Catholicism, mainstream Protestantism, and Reformed Judaism could live together with modern science, while "Orthodox Jews and fundamentalist Protestants and Muslims . . . have still not made their accommodations. . . ." From my experience, even the most Orthodox of Jews have been able to make their peace with science. It is the small group of the ultra-Orthodox, both in the United States and in Israel, who insist on a literal interpretation of each word of the Bible.

The clearest expression of Sagan's thinking on Judaism can be found in his essay in the collected work titled *The Jewish Condition,* a group of essays on contemporary Judaism that were collected to honor Rabbi Alexander Schindler when he retired as president of the Union of American Hebrew Congregations. In Rabbi Schindler's introduction to Sagan's article, he admonishes his fellow Jews to give a Jewish response to "the degradation of God's creation. The place on which we stand, this planet Earth, is holy, and we must never countenance its despoilation." In his essay titled "Religious Leadership and Environmental Integrity," Sagan writes:

> I have long admired Rabbi Schindler for his concern for justice, for the depth of his knowledge, for his kindly demeanor, and for his courage. How many Jewish leaders urge their fellow rabbis to stop romanticizing Orthodoxy? Where it alone prevails . . . stale repression, fossilized tradition, and ethical corruption often hold sway. And so it is not surprising that Rabbi Schindler, almost alone among the religious leaders, has had the courage to state forthrightly what one of the major impediments is in repairing the environment, on which all of us depend. . . . Schindler stated that our recent ecological disasters are the price of profit, the price of corporate thinking about human values, the price of a materialism so corrosive that it can rupture an oil tanker's hull. . . . We agreed that the ecological crisis hovers over our many other vital concerns since the threat to the environment is global, endangering all human life. . . .

Just about the same time that Carl Sagan contributed to the volume on Rabbi Schindler, his new book was published titled *Science as a Candle in the Dark: The Demon-Haunted World.* Much of this more personal book is devoted to critiquing pseudoscientific faith healing, claims of visiting aliens, and other strange phenomena. Yet he has sections that warmly describe his parents who, though not rich, always had the greatest understanding and encouragement for his scholastic endeavors. He remembers his parents lovingly as if they were still alive. I would have felt better to know that this world renowned scientist was willing to mention the spiritual guidance he received from his parents. Sagan had theological discussions with religious leaders like the Buddhist Dalai Lama, and he read Moses Maimonides' *Guide for the Perplexed.* But the clearest presentation of his views on Judaism remains that one contribution to the volume dedicated to Rabbi Schindler.

🐜   🐜   🐜

On a recent ABC news program, Peter Jennings told about a Southern Baptist Convention at which one of the leaders informed the audience about their goal: to convert their "friends" the Jews to Christianity. Rabbi James Rudin of the American Jewish Committee responded by saying that this Baptist statement had set back the Jewish-Christian understanding for hundreds of years. Rabbi Rudin's response surprised the Baptist minister, since his denomination had tried similar conversion efforts for as long as he could remember. Come to think of it, is it not more human (not to mention more humane) to destroy the Jewish people by conversion than through another pogrom?

In this connection it is time to discuss Dr. Laura Schlessinger's best-selling work *How Could You Do That!* She is a psychologist licensed in marriage and family therapy with a radio audience of millions of listeners each week. I first heard her program when she was a guest of Dr. Robert Schuller. She told of coming from a traditional Jewish household. Naturally, she has no argument with anybody of another religious or nonreligious persuasion, but she stresses the values of the Hebrew Scriptures as they were taught in the Bible for the first time and taught over the centuries to all the people of the world.

"There is something that separates human beings from being too simply categorized as yet another animal," she writes, "and that something is morality." The author stresses the three Cs: character, courage, and conscience. In the numerous responses to her clients, who talk about their marriages and family situations, doing what they like to do but not what they ought to do, Dr. Schlessinger writes: "There is a profound difference between doing what feels good right now and doing what you know to be morally incorrect right now. . . . The former results in a temporary thrill (if you are lucky) but not in long-term positive feeling about oneself. The latter results in a temporary frustration (a tough challenge) and a long-term positive feeling about the self."

In a Postscript, after having described many case histories, Dr. Schlessinger explains once again the concept of maintaining personal integrity by quoting from the Bible (or Tanakh). She cites the well-known words God is believed to have spoken to Cain, who didn't do what is right:

> Why are you so distressed,
> And why is your face fallen?
> Surely if you do right,
> There is an uplift.
> But if you do not do right
> Sin couches at the door;
> Its urge is toward you,
> Yet, you can be its master.

"It seems to me," Dr. Schlessinger concludes, "that God is teaching us that joy comes from doing 'right' in spite of the reactions from or input by others."

A more specific treatment of the God of Judaism has been offered under the title *God: A Biography* by Jack Miles, director of the Humanities Center at Claremont Graduate School, near Los Angeles. He is also a contributing editor to *Atlantic Monthly.* The author, a former Jesuit, took religious instruction at the Pontifical Gregorian University of Rome and at Hebrew University in Jerusalem. He lives with his wife and daughter in Southern California.

Miles's research has been done with the help of the Hebrew Bible instead of the Christianized Old Testament. *God: A Biography,* which won the Pulitzer Prize, has been on the *New York Times* best-seller list since it came out in hardcover, continues to be a best seller in paperback, and has received glowing reviews everywhere. Paul Johnson, author of *The History of Christianity, A History of the Jews,* and more recently *A Quest for God,* summarized his views of Miles's book in *Commentary* magazine: "No summary of mine can do justice to the richness of this book."

The reason for all of this praise becomes clear if we follow this unusual biography of the God of our Bible. We are reminded again and again how the God who gave us the Ten Commandments has been acting like a warrior and has been responsible for the death of human beings. For centuries more and more famous people have discussed the Book of Job in which God tested Job by taking all of his possessions away, even his children. But Job remained upright. Job argued with God, maintaining that he had suffered innocently, but God gave him a very unsatisfactory answer.

What a relief it is to read in Leviticus these eternal words: "When a stranger resides with you in your land, you shall not wrong him. The stranger who resides with you shall be to you as one of your citizens; you shall love him as yourself, for you were strangers in the land of Egypt."

How can we explain this discrepancy between the two views of God in the Old Testament? Conservative and Reformed Jews do not believe in the literal interpretation of the Bible. They also believe in stages of spiritual development, from very simple religious conceptions to the heights of prophetic Judaism. We know, of course, what to accept as we read Deuteronomy: "Surely this instruction which I enjoin upon you this day is not too baffling for you, nor is it beyond reach. It is not in the heavens, that you should say, 'Who among us can go up to the heavens and get it for us and impart it to us, that we may observe it?' "

I am sure that the majority of the Jewish people will discard any commandments in the Hebrew Bible with which they disagree. We find, on the other hand, such high ideals in our Book of Books, ideals that will not be reached until the end of time. And it is Jack Miles's marvelous book that leads us back to the Hebrew Scriptures.

🐾   🐾   🐾

At the age of twenty-six Dennis Prager, together with his friend Joseph Telushkin, wrote one of the basic books about the Jewish people—*The Nine Questions People Ask about Judaism.* In the last issue of *Ultimate Issues* he wrote about 'The Present State of My Jewish Beliefs." Essentially, he is saying that "The Torah is divine. . . . This does not necessarily mean that God wrote every word of it." When asked if his beliefs had changed since he wrote the book with Joseph Telushkin, Prager said that he never wavered in his belief that the Hebrew Bible is the original truth and that Jews should never waver in their covenant with God. He still believes "that the Jewish people have a God-given mission to humanity." On the other hand, he has changed quite positively in his belief that other religions have divine truth. "First, because during ten years of weekly interfaith dialogue I had met too many beautiful, God-fearing members of other faiths whose decency and piety came from their religious beliefs. Second, because it became inconceivable to me that God made revelation accessible only to one tenth of one percent of mankind."

There was yet another definite change in Prager. His synagogue of regular attendance is no longer Orthodox, "because after forty-three years trying to love Orthodox services, I felt another forty-three years of trying would prove fruitless." He came to an important conclusion while thinking about the present state of Jewish beliefs. He makes a sharp distinction between the Hebrew Bible (the Tanakh) or written law and the rabbinical laws, which have to be changed in important instances. His reasoning is that "the written law is to be regarded as permanent and that the purpose of the oral law is to continuously reinterpret the written." Prager concludes his remarks by saying "I have come to believe that the most important effort to be made in Judaism is developing vibrant non-Orthodox religiosity."

❧   ❧   ❧

Here I must mention a book that came out in 1996 and is surely a "must read" for anyone who wants to explore the Hebrew Bible. It is Lillian Freudmann's book *What's in the Bible?* She had written her first book, *Anti-Semitism in the New Testament,* two years before. Trained as a social worker, she served in Israel as a case worker for new immigrants. She has also taught courses in Hebrew, Bible Studies, and Jewish subjects at University of Connecticut's School of Continuing Education and elsewhere.

In this concise look at the thirty-nine books of the Hebrew Bible, Freudmann explains how challenging and intimidating the Book of Books can be for readers. Some get discouraged in their studies and "give up in despair."

The books of the Bible consist of five books of Moses, the twenty-one books of the Prophets, and the thirteen Ketuvim or Holy writings (Psalms, Proverbs, Job, Daniel, Ezra, Nehemiah, First and Second Chronicles, and the five scrolls— Song of Songs, Ruth, Lamentations, Ecclesiastes, and Esther). These books are summarized by the author so that "readers of the Bible can understand the plot or story line of each book. . . . Once readers. . .are familiar with the contents, they will feel more comfortable about delving into the Book of Books." What a simple, straightforward approach that makes understanding the Hebrew Bible more of an adventure than a task.

I had planned to end my discussion of Judaism and the Bible at this point but then I received a copy of *Commentary* only to find a symposium titled "What Do Jews Believe?" Forty-seven heads of rabbinical seminaries, congregational rabbis, scholars, and professors were questioned on such mat-

ters as: Do you believe in God? Do you believe the Torah to
be divine revelation? . . . In what sense do you believe the
Jews are the chosen people of God? . . . How have . . . the
Holocaust and the existence of the state of Israel influenced
you. . .? Do you see any prospect of a large-scale revival of
Judaism in America?"

Exactly thirty years ago *Commentary* carried a symposium
under the title "The State of Jewish Belief," in which four of
the previous contributors to the most recent article also participated. The interviewed scholars belonged to all branches of
the Jewish faith—Orthodox, Conservative, and Reformed or
Reconstructionist movements. These periodic assessments
give Jews and non-Jews a nonbinding selection of well-rea-
soned views to consider and reflect upon. It is interesting to
keep these issues of *Commentary* from year to year just to see
how much ideas and arguments change and how much they
remain the same. The feminist readers should be pleased to see
that many more women are being asked to give their thoughts
on the state of Jewish beliefs.

20

New Beginnings

I would like to end this volume with an event that I surely consider one of the most important chapters of my life. I reported with much pride and honor in chapter 13 that the Shoah Visual History Foundation, founded and chaired by producer/director Steven Spielberg, contacted me to solicit my participation in the videotaping of testimonies of those who survived the Holocaust. This project is more urgent now than ever before since fewer and fewer survivors are left. With Spielberg's help, those of us remaining can contribute in creating a video archive of memories and impressions to make sure that one of the most devastating events in human history is never forgotten and never repeated.

In a city the size of Syracuse (unlike larger metropolitan areas such as New York City, Los Angeles, San Francisco, Miami, or Chicago) not too many Holocaust survivors remain, and not many volunteers had yet been trained to videotape the testimonies of survivors in these smaller communities. I was pleased therefore to receive a call in July of 1996 from a young lady named Jane Greenberg of Ithaca, New York, who made an appointment to interview me for the Shoah Foundation. She was a special education teacher who was doing post-graduate work at Cornell University.

On her first visit, she discussed with me in depth our family's suffering during the terror of the Third Reich. We reviewed in detail which documents I had been given by the Nazis. I also found the originals of some of the copies I had located, so everything was ready when Ms. Greenberg returned a week later with Mr. Slawomir, the cameraman, and his assistant Jason. I showed Ms. Greenberg the documents I received from the Red Cross Tracing Center stating that my elderly parents and Herta's mother were deported by the Nazis to Theresienstadt and probably sent from there to one of the extermination camps. The tracing center had no knowledge of my sister, Kaete's, fate.

I showed the cameraman a picture of my wedding in 1938 for videotaping and the infamous statement by the German ministry that I had fulfilled all of my requirements for a license to practice medicine in Germany, except one—being of Aryan descent. And I found the original card I had sent to Herta; my parents; and my sister in Breslau from the concentration camp in Buchenwald, where I was incarcerated just two weeks after my wedding and where I was held as a prisoner for six weeks before I was able to emigrate with Herta to the United States. It was the only time we were allowed to send a message from Buchenwald to our homes in Nazi Germany. We were told exactly what to write: "We are sitting here and are well. Don't write, as there is shutting off of mail at present." The rest of my immediate family was also interviewed by the camera crew and Ms. Greenberg.

Jane Greenberg asked me in her interview how I would summarize my experience as a Holocaust survivor. In answer to such an emotionally charged question, I recited a poem I had composed in 1963, after returning with Herta from a visit to our relatives in California. I read it from a copy of *Once a Doctor, Always a Doctor*:

Returning East on the crowded train,
The Central New York ride was not in vain.
We met a poet, we met a nun,
And we had certainly lots of fun.
The poet said to the nun in her robe—
While discussing the merits of John, the late pope—
That he, although being a Protestant,
Had worked with Catholics hand in hand;
And he found this meeting an occasion,
To stress again his admiration.
The nun, she answered with a smile so big:
"Then you know that I am a Catholic?"
She also declared in that train-dining-hall,
That, wearing her robe, was no hardship at all.
In contrast to other girls, she has never to guess,
What hat she should wear or what kind of dress.
We Jews at the table found here proof to the rumor,
That true religion shows a keen sense of humor.
And somewhere we saw some hopeful rays
Of understanding in future days.
The reader should not consider a crime,
That some of my sentences do not rhyme.
I am not a poet, as you can see,
But just an ordinary M.D.
Best wishes to Buddhists, Christians, and Jews.
To all, from Heinz Hartmann in Syracuse.

I also read from my autobiography the much-quoted saying from Pastor Martin Niemoeller, who resisted the Nazis and was incarcerated in a concentration camp himself: "At first the Nazis went after the Jews, but I was no Jew, and I didn't speak up. Then they went after the Catholics, but I was no Catholic and remained silent. Then they went after the trade unionists, but I was no trade unionist and did not say anything. Finally, they came after me, and there was nobody left to speak out anymore."

About six weeks after the interview, I received my own copy of the videotape from Universal Pictures, together with a letter from Steven Spielberg. They had indeed used the picture of my wedding and a photo of my sister-in-law Lucy van der Linde (age ninety-two) I know Lucy certainly wants to be interviewed by the Shoah Foundation at her home in Sunnyvale, California. Fortunately, Lucy was never incarcerated in a concentration camp, but her experience was nonetheless terribly frightening. She and her five children were hidden from the Nazis. They were all given false identity papers and endured terrible illness and starvation while in hiding. Just before the end of the war in Germany, Lucy was tremendously afraid of being discovered. Luckily, she was saved when American troops marched in. The rumble and shooting of the liberating army sounded to her like music from heaven.

The videotape also dealt with my other surviving relatives: Eric and Inge Spitz and their families in Toronto, Canada. There was also a picture of cousin Eric's sister Uschi and her husband, Johnny, originally from England. They also lived for decades with their immediate families in Toronto.

        &   **&**   **&**

How sad I was to receive a call from Dr. Jenny Preuss, daughter of my lifelong friend Dr. Fred S. Preuss, informing me that he had suddenly passed away. He, too, was pictured on the Shoah videotape. He had been able to emigrate to the United States from Breslau about two years before I received my own U.S. Visa. He was able at first to persuade one of my older female cousins in San Francisco to overcome her initial reluctance and to sponsor Herta and me with her affidavit. After arrangements had been made for our voyage on the Swedish-American ocean liner, Fred, together with my brother-in-law, Herbert, paid our passage in U.S. dollars thereby enabling us to get out of Nazi Germany. Fred literally saved our lives!

        &   **&**   **&**

Just a few words about my health. I remain on the coronary reversal treatment for my blocked arteries, under the direction and care of Dr. Lance Gould. In summer, with the frequent high humidity—especially at night—I experience many more angina attacks. To control for the attacks I would take 40 mg of Isordil every four hours, but my doctors placed me on a Nitro-Patch before bedtime for more efficient control of the angina.

When September came we hoped that the cooler weather would moderate the attacks but they still occurred day and night. Finally, Dr. Gould called to talk to me personally about my condition in the hope of getting to the root of the problem. He could not understand the frequency of the attacks. At one point he even doubted that I was having them and was concerned that the Nitrostat therapy had failed. Then he remembered that I was still on 5 mg of Norvasc, a calcium channel blocker prescribed for my hypertension. It has a common side effect of increasing the frequency and intensity of angina. Dr. Gould discontinued the Norvasc and in no time the chest pains diminished. In the cold and moist autumn weather in central New York the humidity might reach ninety percent or higher on those days, even with the reduced levels of Norvasc, my chest discomfort is still present.

I continue to take my beta carotene, vitamin C (1000 mg) vitamin E, and Propanolol (or Inderal), to keep my pulse at a slower rate. My blood pressure is quite well controlled with the small dose of Vasotec. And I remain on 20 mg of Zorcor, one of the most reliable anticholesterol drugs and one that I have been taking since starting on the reversal diet.

    🐜   🐜   🐜

I was pleased to receive a call recently from Dr. Frederick Roberts, the pediatrician who took care of our son, Michael, as well as my daughter, Joan, and both of my grandchildren. In discussing our separate lives, the status of Michael's condition, and other matters, I was happy to learn that Dr. Robert's autobiography about his many years in pediatric practice would be published soon.

&   &   &

Returning for a moment to the role of Judaism in the world and the relations of the Jews to the Bible, people frequently tell me that the Bible is full of contradictions, that they don't understand it, or that they are just so busy with work or their home life that they can't seem to read it. Well, I may have a partial solution.

I recommend Lillian Freudmann's learned book *What's in the Bible?* with its synopses of the thirty-nine books of the Hebrew Bible, in which we find in the Torah, centuries before Rabbi Hillel, the Book of Leviticus (about 1450 B.C.E.) the following admonitions: Love your neighbor as yourself; be respectful to old people; treat the stranger the same way as the citizen by having the same laws for both aliens and natives, and don't deceive the former.

This is what Rabbi Hertz, the late chief rabbi of the British empire (and at one time rabbi of Temple Adath Yeshurun in Syracuse), has to say in his translation of the Pirke Aboth (or *Sayings of the Fathers*): "Sayings of the Fathers is the most widely known tract of the Mishna," which is almost entirely concerned with moral conduct. We have already discussed the teachings of the fundamental love of ones neighbor. This is what Joseph Hertz tells us about the Golden Rule in Judaism: "The world at large is unaware of the fact that the sublime maxim of morality, 'Thou shall love your neighbor as yourself (Leviticus 19:18) was first taught by Judaism. No less a thinker than John Stuart Mill expressed his surprise that it came from the Pentateuch."

&   &   &

I have in front of me the September 1, 1996 edition of the *Prager Perspective,* edited by Dennis Prager. In his article,

Prager quoted an earlier *New York Times* report stating that "The Tennessee senate has approved by a vote of 27 to 1 a resolution urging homes, businesses, places of worship, and schools to post and observe the Ten Commandments." A little later in the report it states, "State Senator Steve Cohen . . . the Senate's only Jewish member . . . was the only Senator to vote against the resolution." Senator Cohen explained his vote by saying that "the religious right has many people crippled and blinded."

Dennis Prager explains in his article that the Tennessee Senate passed no law: "it merely encourages Tennessee citizens to heed and to post the Ten Commandments. The citizens are completely free to ignore the Senate's encouragement." There is no question about separation of church and state here. "The Jews," according to the late Jewish philosopher Abraham Heschel's words "are a messenger who forgot his message."

The article in the September issue of the *Prager Perspective* was titled "The Ten Commandments: Given by Ancient Jews, Removed by Modern Jews." Some readers sent this article to State Senator Cohen of Tennessee, who was anxious to debate the issue with Dennis Prager, and the following day they debated for two hours on Prager's radio show. The debate was edited and reprinted in the October 1, issue of the *Prager Perspective.* I still think that the twenty-seven members of the Tennessee State Senate who passed the resolution were right "to encourage every citizen of Tennessee to observe the Ten Commandments, teach them to their children, and display them in their homes, businesses, schools, and places of work." We have seen that the Golden Rule is the basic teaching of Judaism, and the Ten Commandments are an essential feature of our Hebrew Bible. "The rest is commentary," as Rabbi Hillel would say.

How do we love our neighbor? Where do we look for commentary? To me and so many others the Pirke Avot comes to mind, whether in Rabbi Hertz's translation or the more recent one by the United American Hebrew Congregations. These *Sayings of the Fathers* are modern commentary on

Jewish ethics and are the most well known of all writings in rabbinical Judaism. It is one of the tracts of the Mishnah, compiled in the early third century of the common era." It has been a favorite text of many Jews and was originally part of regular Sabbath readings:

> Ben Zoma said: "Who is wise? The one who learns from everyone.
>> Who is mighty? One who controls his natural urges.
>> Who is rich? One who is happy with what he has.
>> Who is honored? One who honors others."

Recommended Reading

Allen, Steve. *Steve Allen on the Bible, Religion, and Morality.* Amherst, N.Y.: Prometheus Books, 1990.
Aufbau, 2121 Broadway, New York, N.Y. 10023.

Batzdorff, Susanne M. *Edith Stein: Selected Writings.* Springfield, Ill.: Templegate Publishers, 1990.
Broyard, Anatole. *Intoxicated by My Illness.* New York: Clarkson Potter Publishers, 1992.

Cohn-Sherbok, Dan. *Not a Job for a Nice Jewish Boy.* London: Bellow Publishing, 1993.
Coles, Robert. *The Spiritual Life of Children.* Boston: Houghton-Mifflin Company, 1990.
Commentary magazine. 165 East 56th Street, New York, 10022.

Dan, Bruce E. and Roxanne K. Young. *A Piece of My Mind.* Feeling Fine Programs, Inc., 1998.

Encyclopedia Judaica, 16 vols., Jerusalem: Keter, and New York: Macmillan, 1972 (decennial volume, 1982).

Frankl, Vicktor. *Man's Search for Meaning.* New York: Washington Square Press, 1963.
Freudmann, Lillian C. *What's in the Bible?* Northvale, N.J.: Jason Aronson Inc., 1996.

Gellman, Rabbi Marc and Monsignor Thomas Hartman. *How Do You Spell God?* New York: Morrow Junior Books, 1995.
————. *Where Does God Live?* New York: Triumph Books, 1991.
Goldberger, Leo. *The Rescue of the Danish Jews.* New York: New York University Press, 1987.
Gould, Allan. *What Did They Think of the Jews.* Northvale, N.J.: Jason Aronson, Inc., 1991.

Hartmann, Heinz., M.D. *Once a Doctor, Always a Doctor.* Amherst, N.Y.: Prometheus Books, 1986.
Hertz, Rabbi Joseph H. *Sayings of the Fathers.* West Orange, N.J.: Behrman House, 1945.

John Paul II (pope). *Crossing the Threshold of Hope.* New York: Alfred A. Knopf, Inc., 1994.

Kaminsky, Alice R. *The Victim's Song.* Amherst, N.Y.: Promtheus Books, 1985.
Kaufman, Jonathan. *Broken Alliance.* New York: Charles Scribner's Sons, 1988.
Keneally, Thomas. *Schlinder's List.* New York: Penguin Books, 1982.
Klagsburn, Francine. *Voices of Wisdom.* New York: Pantheon, 1980.
Kravitz, Leonard, and Kerry M. Olitzky. *Pirke Avot.* New York: UAHC Press, 1993.
Kurtz, Paul. *In Defense of Secular Humanism.* Amherst, N.Y.: Prometheus Books, 1983.

Kurtz, Paul. *Living Without Religion.* Amherst, N.Y.: Prometheus Books, 1994.

Kushner, Harold. *When Bad Things Happen to God People.* New York: Schocken Books, 1981.

Lester, Julius. *Lovesong: Becoming a Jew.* New York: Henry-Holt and Company, 1988.

Miles, Jack. *God: A Biography.* New York: Vintage Books, 1995.

Newman, Judith Sternberg. *In the Hell of Auschwitz.* Smithtown, N.Y.: Exposition Press, 1978.

Prager, Dennis, and Joseph Telushkin. *The Nine Questions People Ask about Judaism.* New York: Simon and Schuster, 1975.

Randi, James. *The Faith Healers.* Amherst, N.Y. Prometheus Books, 1987.

———. *Flim Flam!* Amherst, N.Y.: Prometheus Books, 1982.

Riemer, Jack. *Wrestling with the Angel.* New York: Schocken Books, 1995.

Romanoff, Lena, with Lisa Hostein. *Your People, My People.* New York: The Jewish Publication Society, 1990.

Rubenstein, Richard T. *After Auschwitz.* New York: Bobbs-Merrill Company, Inc., 1966.

Scalamonti, John David. *Ordained to Be a Jew.* Hoboken, N.J.: KTAV Publishing House, Inc., 1992.

Schlessinger, Laura. *How Could You Do That!* New York: HarperCollins, 1996.

Siegel, Bernie S., M.D. *Love, Medicine, and Miracles.* New York: Harper and Row, 1986.

Simons, Howard. *Jewish Times.* Boston: Houghton-Mifflin Company, 1988.

Sonsino, Rifat, and Daniel B. Syme. *Finding God.* Northvale, N.J.: Jason Aronson Inc., 1986.

Sonsino, Rifat. *Why I Am a Reform Jew.* New York: Donald I. Fine, Inc., 1989.

Stein, Edith. *Life in a Jewish Family.* Washington, D.C.: ICS Publications, 1986.

Szasz, Suzy. *Living With It.* Amherst, N.Y.: Prometheus Books, 1991.

Szasz, Thomas S., M.D. *The Therapeutic State.* Amherst, N.Y.: Prometheus Books, 1984.

Telushkin, Rabbi Joseph. *Jewish Literacy.* New York: William Morrow and Company, Inc., 1991.

Weisel, Elie. *Memoirs: All Rivers Run to the Sea.* New York: Alfred A. Knopf, 1995.

————. *Messengers of God.* New York: Random House, 1976.

Wolff, Tobias. *This Boy's Life.* New York: Harper and Row, 1989.

Wolpe, David J. *Teaching Your Children about God.* New York: Henry Holt and Company, 1993.